I Want My Life To Matter

The
C.A.R.E.
Principle

Creating a Life That Makes a Difference to
the World When You're Under Thirty

Brandon Gaydorus

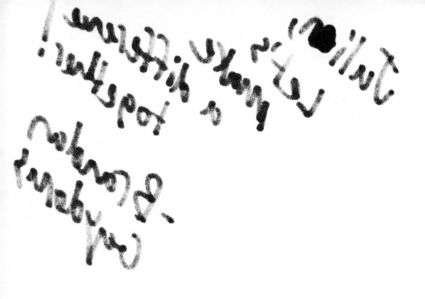

ISBN: 9781656740311

DEDICATION

This book is dedicated to everyone that has helped me out and to all the mentors out there who make time to spread their knowledge to others.

CONTENTS

The Stories
Creating Opportunities

Welcoming

Open-Minded

Consistency

Ten Concepts Toward Consistency and Fulfillment:

Respect

Growth

Greatness

Having Fun

ACKNOWLEDGMENTS

Thank you to my mentors, friends, and family who have helped me put together the stories, values, and ideas to develop *The C.A.R.E. Principle*.

INTRODUCTION

The purpose of this book is to inspire you to create opportunities and make things happen. In high school, I worked in an assisted living home and it became clear to me that, at the end of life, those who seem happiest have few or no regrets. If you give your all in life, influence people, strive to make the world a better place, and go after what you want with your **health**, **wealth**, **relationships**, and **happiness**, it is hard to believe you would have many regrets.

There are going to be ups and downs, peaks and valleys, celebrations and times of humility. But what if all of those lead to something special, something great, and something that makes your life of meaning?

Two people I look up to for how they took advantage of their time on Earth are Jerry Weintraub and Jim Rohn.

Jerry lived a life filled with persistence from taking Elvis Presley and Frank Sinatra on tour, to producing the *Karate Kid*, to even becoming an actor in *Ocean's Thirteen*. His legacy lives on through his documentary, movies, and book about his life (*When I Stop Talking, You'll Know I'm Dead*).

Jim faced financial adversity early in life before meeting one of his mentors whose influence helped him earn his first million dollars. He eventually went to teach thousands (maybe millions) of people how to achieve financial freedom in their own lives.

Though both of these men have passed away, they have had a massive influence on my desire to share these concepts and stories through writing.

The book splits up into four categories that represent core values. Values that, if embraced, will lead to a life of meaning and minimal regrets. These concepts came from influential mentors, real-life situations, and impactful books.

The four core values are:

CREATE OPPORTUNITIES
- For you and others through being **welcoming**, **open-minded**, and through **unforgettable experiences**.

ACTIVE LIFESTYLE
- Living this lifestyle through **leading by example**, **positivity**, and **consistency**.

RESPECT IS EARNED
- Understanding that it's not always just given. It can be earned in many ways, especially through **loyalty**, **being present**, and **taking ownership**.

EXCELLING FORWARD
- By accelerating forward to get what you want and where you want to be through **growth**, **greatness**, and by **having fun**.

The first letters of the core values spell a word reflecting the main trait of the most impactful leaders.

- Think of a family member that you've always looked up to.

- Think of Martin Luther King Jr. and what he did for the African-American community.

- Think of Mother Theresa and what she did for the lower class.

- Think of Abe Lincoln and how he helped save the Union and free slaves.

When these people come to mind, you may agree the one word to describe each leader would be that they...

CARE

If you **care** about helping people and living a life of meaning, these four values and their twelve sub-values will help get you there.

To get the most out of the stories in the book, put yourself in the shoes of the character in the story, and then relate it to an event in your life.

What would you do?

Why would you do it?

How could you use this concept to improve?

CREATE OPPORTUNITIES

How to Get Whatever You Want

One question everyone seems to want to know the answer to is…

How do I get whatever I want?

The answer is…ASK!

Jim Rohn is famous for explaining this concept. He mentions that the Bible says, "Ask…and you shall receive."

Asking starts a process to help attract answers, which can lead to created opportunities. The art of 'asking' applies to all aspects of life…

*

If you want a boyfriend or girlfriend, what do you do?

You start asking people for their names.

You start asking people if they know anybody who may be interested.

You start asking couples you admire what makes their relationship work and what they like about each other.

And you start getting answers to move you forward.

*

With your wealth, if you want a job or to get raise, what do you do?

You start asking, what do I have to do to get a raise?

What credentials do I need?

*

With your health, if you want to be in better shape or improve your eating habits, what do you do?

You start asking people who are in the shape you want. What are you doing? What's working with your workouts and nutrition?

*

When you start asking, you start receiving, and opportunities will begin to arise.

***

Introducing Yourself to Someone You Like May Be the Best Compliment You Can Give!

It's a typical afternoon in college, and you're enjoying dinner at the dining hall. After grabbing your plate and turning to your left, you notice someone you like across the room. Without much thought, you walk over confidently, shake the hand of the person you're attracted to, and then ask for his or her name. You give a compliment or crack a funny joke and walk away. The other person is shocked and thrown off, but can't seem to get you off their mind.

Why is this?

It is because going up to someone you like may be the best

compliment you can give. The person who gets approached knows why you're introducing yourself, and whether they want to talk to you or not, they're smiling inside knowing you gave him/or her attention and had enough confidence to go up and say hello. What you say initially is almost always irrelevant, but a confident and authentic approach will help set a spark for a future relationship.

Remember, no one has ever made a shot they didn't take.

***

Bringing Value to Find an Unexpected Workout Partner

It's party time, and your friend is throwing a top-five party of the year. You're enjoying life with a cold drink in your hand and embracing the positive vibes of the great people around you!

As you're sitting there, watching a game of beer pong, there is one thing in the back of your mind, that you can't get over.

It's your "beer gut" that has been coming into form lately. It's been frustrating and has made you feel sensitive about your weight. Over to your left, there is someone who's in great shape and smiling bright with confidence, and it looks like this guy's nickname could be "The Health Nut."

With enough courage finally built up, you ask him how he stays in such great shape. He immediately shrugs you off thinking you've had too much to drink and that you're just playing games.

But since you're determined to make a change, his lack of acknowledgment doesn't phase you, and you go right back up to him and say:

"What do I need to do to get in shape like you? I'm serious, and I could use any advice you can give me."

He can now see the intense look in your eye. The look that reminded him of himself before getting help on his health journey years ago.

He decides to test you and says, "Meet me at the gym on Monday at 6 AM, and you can work out with me."

Monday morning comes around, and there you are ready to go. Throughout the workout, you work hard and stay positive. The Health Nut tells you how he appreciated that and invites you back.

The next workout, you show up, bring the energy, and crush it. The Health Nut decides he could use a workout partner to help spot weight and give him an extra push. He sees the value you bring and asks you to become his permanent workout partner.

You created an opportunity for yourself to learn from one of the best and receive help to make this positive change, maybe even get in the best shape of your life.

***

Building a Network – Would You Rather Have a Billion Friends or a Billion Dollars?

Are opportunities a matter of being in the right place at the right time? A matter of luck?

Or

Are they the result of the preparation established before the opportunities were present? A matter of knowing the right people? Of continuously solving problems?

*

It's August, school starts up in two weeks, and you're poolside enjoying the closing days of summer. As you're lying down, flipping through a magazine, one page sticks out with the question, "Would you rather have a billion dollars or a billion friends?"

After thinking about this all day, you think: Why not a billion dollars? You'd be able to retire for the rest of your life.

Later in the article, the author gives you his take by saying if you have a billion "solid" friends and asked all of them for $10, you'd have ten billion dollars.

A network of people can lead to more opportunities, that can increase your wealth at a faster rate.

With that said, would you agree that increasing your network should be a high priority? If yes, why?

_____

_____

_____

***

Search for New Opportunities

PEOPLE = OPPORTUNITIES

An essential concept of this book is to understand:

"Where there are people, there are opportunities."

Take time to think about where you can find the people who will help get you to where you want to be?

Are they...

At meetings? At social events? At work? At seminars? At big events like concerts, the Super Bowl, the Masters, or the World Cup?

Take two minutes to write down five places you can go to meet people you'd like to be like, or who can help you grow with your health, wealth, and/or relationships.

1.) _____
    _____

2.) _____
    _____

3.) _____
    _____

4.) _____
    _____

5.) _____
    _____

When you go to these places, engage in conversations, be curious, and look for answers/opportunities.

Welcoming

The More You Take Care of People, the More they Take Care of You

The school year is ending, and it's time to spend the summer on Cape Cod experiencing new things and learning from your internship.

Since your 9-5 internship is paying next to nothing, you decide to get a job at the local ice cream shop. It's a place that will be busy at night, has the potential for tip money, and gives you free ice cream at the end shifts!

After getting trained at the ice cream shop, the manager sits down with you to explain what makes this shop different from the others. Your manager says...

1.) We serve the best damn ice cream there is.

And

2.) We make our customers feel welcome...
   - By remembering their names
   - By knowing their go-to choices
   - By greeting each customer with a warm welcome and leaving them with a kind goodbye, to ensure that customers have a positive experience.

After the two-minute meeting, your manager says, "That's all for today. Welcome to the team if you have any problems, questions, or issues, please don't hesitate to inform me."

You say, "That's it?" and your boss says, "Yes, that's it. Follow those two rules, and you'll do well."

After the meeting, cleanup and everyday duties still have to be finished, but it becomes apparent if those two rules are followed, the business will run well.

Working your first Friday night is a blur. Customer's come in and out throughout the shift, along with non-stop ice cream scooping and endless smiling to keep people happy. Before leaving, you get handed $100 in tips from the manager! Four hours of work, and you've got $100 on top of your wages.

It's incredible what being welcoming and providing quality customer service can do!

Scooping ice cream all summer provides you with enough income to buy groceries and have some spending money at night. That summer, you learned more on your "side job" than you did filing papers at your internship.

You learned that the more you take care of people, the more they take care of you.

***

The Cute Dog That Makes Your Day

It's a long line as you wait to get through airport security. You're starving, dehydrated, anxious, and in an awful mood when the guy behind you accidentally steps on the heel of your foot. Your cheeks turn red; pissed off describes the look on your face perfectly, and you're ready to pull this guy's hair out!

After taking a deep breath, calming down, and looking away, you see a cute little dog staring you down. Not barking, biting, or being disruptive in any way. All you can think of is how you want to pet the dog and let him lick your fingers. You ask the lady with the dog if you can say hi and pet him. Of course, she says yes! Your day just got made, everything negative from earlier has left your mind, and the plane ride back is as chill as an igloo in Alaska.

Is the attitude shift just because the dog was there? Or is this because the dog is approachable, friendly, and means well (or at least appears to).

What if you were as approachable as the dog? Would more people talk to you? Why or why not?

_____

_____

What does being "welcoming" mean to you?

_____

_____

***

Knowing Names Sets You Apart

It's been a tough day at work, so tough that going outside for fresh air is a necessity right now. After walking a couple of blocks, out of the blue, someone calls your name: "Blake, Blake, Blake!"

Naturally, your response is to look over and see who the heck is calling your name. It turns out to be someone from last week's luncheon at work. You met this person briefly and had an okay conversation (from what you remember). But what can't seem to leave your mind is that this person remembered your name after one conversation! This brings a smile to your face, increases your interest to keep talking, and it helps you forget about all the annoying crap that happened earlier today.

*

Remembering and stating someone's name adds a sense of trust, affirmation, and connection that is hard to explain but easy to feel. When you say someone's name, it's like a light bulb turning on in their head, and they are immediately engaged. It's a game-changer, whether your goal is to build a bigger network, to make more money, to retain and gain clients, or to satisfy and grow relationships.

*

Bill Clinton was known to be good at this. He could go into a room with dozens of people he'd never met and shake everyone's hand as he introduced himself one by one to a line of people.

Later in the night, he would tap someone on the shoulder and say their name to start the conversation. Whether he had a system to remember names or asked someone to the left of him what that person's name was, is meaningless.

The point is, he knew that names were important, and he made people feel a sense of trust, affirmation, and connection by stating their name directly to them.

***

The Job That Made You Feel Welcomed

It's winter break, and you're looking for something to do besides drink with your "friends." After asking around, you find out the local country club is hiring temporary employees because of three big events coming up —

Christmas, a couple of weddings, and a massive New Year's Eve party.

Immediately you apply and soon after you get the job. You're required to commit to ten hours of training over three days. Since it's a big club, the manager leaves you with directions for where to meet on the first day of training.

When you arrive for your first day of training, the manager is there to greet you at the door, hands you a name tag, and walks you to a seat. There are a half dozen experienced staff to help with the training, along with a dozen new part-time employees.

Before any work tasks get addressed, the manager calls every new employee up individually to introduce themselves, which helps the team get to know each other better. Then everyone is given a handout with the rules and regulations. The pamphlet includes the following...

- What to wear
- What is "on time"
- Rules and layout of the kitchen
- How to properly pour wine
- Directions on how to serve and set up a plate
- What should not be said to guests
- How to properly show someone where the bathroom is
- What is considered a proper cleanup
- And much more

The expectations set, and training begins.

*

Throughout the training, you're amazed by the team

bonding, expedited learning process, and how excited you are to go to work. The manager made employees feel welcome and set expectations right from the start. You turned a winter break into a valuable life lesson by learning the importance of welcoming experiences and setting clear expectations.

Think back to a time you felt welcomed (at a store, at work, or any random place that fits this concept)…

How did it feel?

_____

_____

What made the experience feel welcoming?

_____

_____

***

The Joy of the Love of Your Life

For this story, think of your parents or a couple that you admire, your current relationship, or what you'd like to have in a future relationship.

*

It's hard to believe that you got married twenty-seven years ago. It was the best day of your life. Good times, good vibes, great people, and a day to celebrate the person you'll be spending the rest of your life with.

The past twenty-seven years have been fantastic. You've raised two kids, put them through college, and helped them find the career of their dreams.

Now in your mid-fifties, you and your other half have settled down with your careers and are in a new phase of life.

Here and there, you still travel for work, and your latest trip was to Chicago. Flying back from the conference, you're excited to come home to your other half.

As you walk through the front door, you get greeted with a hug, a glowing smile, and the best kiss anyone could ask for.

The hug is full of love, the smile shines bright with excitement, and the kiss is full of affection that gives you a tingling feeling from head to toes.

After all these years of marriage, both of you are as excited to see each other as you were twenty-seven years ago.

*

Why is this?

Is it because you've had a long week? Is it because you both committed to each other through thick and thin? Is it because that's what love is? Is it because you both love quality time together?

Or

Is it because you have another opportunity to see, feel, and touch the love of your life? Who would do about anything for you? Who loves seeing you as much as you love seeing them?

*

What do you look for in your future significant other?

Or

If you are in a committed relationship, why do you look forward to seeing him/or her?

_____

_____

What do you or will you need to do to make him/or her want to see you as much as you want to see him/or her?

_____

_____

***

The Art of Smiling

Would you agree that one of the best ways to be welcoming is with a smile?

Whether you're walking by someone at the beach, welcoming a customer at a job, or giving a kind gesture to someone.

Smiling adds a connection with others, positivity to someone's day, and sometimes can even make someone's day.

What if you don't have confidence in your smile?

It's understandable to feel self-conscious about yellow or chipped teeth, white spots, or other dental issues.

Maybe you can try...

1.) Brushing better, flossing consistently, and using mouthwash daily.
2.) If that doesn't work, check out teeth whitening.
3.) If that doesn't work, ask your dentist about implants, crowns, veneers, and other things that can improve your teeth.

If you have crooked teeth, you can look into...

1.) Invisalign or braces.
2.) If that doesn't work, implants and cosmetic work may be an option.

If you have a good smile, great help spread the word about the importance of brushing and taking care of your teeth. This world needs more smiles. Please help spread this message!

It is understandable not to have perfect teeth. If you lack confidence in your smile, then get your teeth fixed. Don't let this affect your life. Smile!

Open-Minded

Maybe Our Parents Were Right

Time feels as if it's flying by now that senior year of college is halfway through. Your friend Joe just got a job offer after college and a big one! $90,000 a year plus benefits. You guys decide to head to the bar for a celebratory shot of tequila.

You're excited for him but a little bummed because you don't have anything set up after college. After your stomach settles down from the nasty shot, out of curiosity, you ask…

"How did you get a job like this?"

Joe: "Since I started college, my parents encouraged me to do internships every summer, to get hands-on experience, and to help me understand what I want to do.

"I was able to save up money from previous internships but, most importantly, build a network of references to help me get this job after college. The people I learned from taught me work ethic, how to take initiative, and helped me progressively develop to put myself in a position to deserve the job I got."

You congratulate Joe and realize, sometimes listening to parents pays off.

***

Getting the Job You Want, Not The Job You Need!

Lying in bed, trying to figure out what the heck you want to do with the rest of your life seems to be a nightly occurrence. Being young, healthy, and willing to do what it takes to be successful (or so you say) has you wondering why you can't seem to figure this out.

*

Chances are you want to do what you want, when you want, with the people you want. Who wouldn't want that?

It is understandable if you don't know what you want. Look at it this way: it makes life more fun and exciting because of the unknown experiences ahead, many of which could be some of the best moments of your life.

When putting together a puzzle, do you know how to solve it right away? Chances are you have no idea, but you know it's possible, leading you to start the puzzle by spreading the pieces on the table and flipping them to the side of the picture.

It's a bigger puzzle than you thought, so you call your friend to come over and help. With the help of your friend, you decide to start building the border (aka the foundation).

Slowly the puzzle gets pieced together. Spots open, pieces connect (through trial and error), and eventually, it's a masterpiece as the puzzle is complete.

The celebration starts by throwing your hands straight up into the air and finishes with the feeling of having accomplished something special.

*

What if the real world worked the same way as the puzzle making process? What if, instead of a puzzle, you thought of someone who had the job you wanted? The puzzle seemed to interest you – what jobs interest you?

*

You've always liked music, so you look up the top record companies, and one in particular sticks out. It's based in NYC and has a couple of hundred employees. After researching the company, you email Human Resources (HR) to see if there are any openings. The HR representative gets back promptly with the link to apply. Suddenly, an opportunity you never thought was possible arises. Excitement is evident as you apply right away. After not hearing back for a week, you email HR to ensure they received your application. They respond to thank you for applying but explain that at this time, you don't fit what they are looking for.

*

Getting turned down hits hard, and locking in a dream job isn't as easy as you thought. Failure, hate, and denial are the storm clouds in your heart as you go to bed that night. After a good night's rest, you realize when you were putting the puzzle together, it took many pieces, many tries, and a lot of effort to connect the right ones to complete the puzzle.

With this thought, a burst of motivation comes, and you decide to call and ask if they would reconsider their decision?

A response comes back your way, and the HR representative is now your most hated person on the planet! She says, "there's nothing open at this time; we will reach out if that changes. Please don't call us back."

*

Two weeks pass. You're still jobless, a month away from graduation, and crossing your fingers for a callback. Later that night, after a few beers, you accept that they are not calling back. It becomes evident that guidance and help are now necessary to get the job you want, and it feels like it needs to be from someone you trust that has experience. Thinking of people to reach out to, your friend's dad comes to mind. He's been the manager at the local grocery store for over fifteen years and has managed and hired hundreds of people.

Since you're away at college, your friend's dad (Harry) agrees to talk to you for fifteen minutes over the phone.

The phone call is set, momentum is going forward (just like early in the puzzle when the border AKA the foundation, starts developing). You prepare a list of questions and excited about the opportunity to talk with someone who has experience in the working world.

In the phone call, Harry expresses one key point: A good boss, a good owner, and a good manager have one key characteristic in common." There's a pause, and you say in your head…

"Yeah, they make a lot of money."

He explains…

"A great leader is always looking for great people.

"If someone wants to work and shows promise, but there isn't a spot open, I find one for him/her. If I can't find a job for him/her, a person of talent will find one for himself or herself. If someone wants a job, all they'd have to do is show value, and openings will arise. Successful businesses are always looking to expand, to grow, and to bring in more revenue. I'm challenging you to find ways to bring value to the company you want to work for and see what happens."

Before the call ends, you ask Harry what he looks for in a good employee and what you need to do to create a job for yourself. He says the following:

- You show up to work with a smile on your face and push aside what is going on outside of work until after your shift. If you had a tough break up, you talk about it after work. If you failed a test at school, you talk about it after work.

- You take initiative. If there is something that needs to be done, you do it, whether it is your job or not. You put grocery carts away that are out of place, you touch up the bathroom every time you go in, and you clean up the eggs that got splattered all over the floor, instead of just walking by like you didn't see them.

- You find solutions to problems. If a lady loses her purse, you help her retrace her steps. If you don't find it, you announce it over the intercom. If that doesn't work, you get more employees to help. If that doesn't work, you look at the video cameras.

- You're fun but productive. Whatever needs to get done, gets done. If it doesn't, then you get it done the next day. Or set up a plan for it to get done.

- You stay open-minded, continue to learn, and have a burning desire to excel and grow.

- You are present and stay in the moment. You give customers and employees your full attention while actively listening, and stay off your phone during work hours.

- You're loyal. You communicate clearly and are honest with feedback. Most importantly, you're authentic.

- You're an action-taker. If something needs to be done, you go do it. You realize, the quicker you do something, the faster it gets done.

- You strive for greatness and realize your work represents the whole company. You know a company is only as strong as its weakest link.

- You're courageous and give people a reason to remember you through your positive work ethic and consistency.

- You can "WOW" the customer through preparation, persistence, and a positive experience that the customer won't forget.

- You take care of your body enough to get the job done effectively and efficiently.

*

After the conversation settles in, your main takeaway is the importance of bringing value to the record company. Leading to the decision that once school finishes, you'll move to NYC near the record company. To pay the bills, you'll find a part-time job waiting tables at night.

*

After making a move to NYC and settling into your place, you decide it's time to pursue the job with the record company. The office opens at 8 AM, so your first move is to show up to the record company the next morning. Since you're excited to show the value you can bring to the company, you show up a quarter to eight with coffee and a smile on your face.

Walking in with a confident stride, you explain to the front desk that the coffee is a delivery for the CEO, Mr. Smith. The person at the front desk says thank you and have a good day. Before walking away, you ask:

Can I bring the coffee to Mr. Smith?

Front Desk: No, he's by appointment only.

Can I schedule an appointment with Mr. Smith?

Front Desk: No, he does not accept walk-in appointments.

Satisfied with your efforts, but disappointed with your results, you take time to think over your encounter on the walk home.

*

After some thought, you decide next time you'll post a note on the coffee with your name, phone number, and why you want to work for the CEO.

The next morning, you drop off the note and coffee to the front desk. Only to get a smile and thank you before getting told to have a good day. Again you ask to meet Mr. Smith but are denied!

You're bummed out but determined to get a job with this company. The next day you do the same thing. Except for this time, you have decided not to leave until Mr. Smith gives you five minutes. As you're patiently waiting, the staff informs you that Mr. Smith isn't here today, and if he were, he would not have the time to meet with you. You say okay, I'll wait here till tomorrow and wait in the office from 8 AM to 5 PM that day, starving and frustrated, and trying to understand why they won't give you a chance. Before you get kicked out at 5 PM, the person at the front desk informs you Mr. Smith wants to meet you tomorrow at 7:55 AM for five minutes.

*

There is hope! The next morning you're taken into Mr. Smith's office. Before you can get a word out, he says:

"Why do you keep asking for me every morning?"

You: "Because I want to work for you, what would that take?"

Mr. Smith: "Okay, I like your determination, but we don't have much open right now."

You: "I understand. How about you let me bring coffee in every morning to you, and I'll clean the toilets after as well."

Mr. Smith: "Boy, you are crazy; see you tomorrow."

Now your foot's in the door, and it's a relief knowing you won't get kicked out in the morning! It's a great feeling, but you understand the goal has not yet been met. Two weeks go by, and you start developing a relationship with Mr. Smith by bringing him coffee every morning. Short, simple, and irrelevant conversations arise. But every weekday morning, the head of the company says your name, you have his attention, and you're what he thinks about at the start of the day.

Before you know it, he starts giving you files to organize, sending you to make copies of documents, along with numbers to call. All of a sudden, you have a job. Not only do you have a job, but you are also now the right-hand man of the person in charge of the entire company! You are now set up to grow, learn, and make money.

Persistence, open-mindedness, and showing value helped lead you to a job you wanted and away from a one you needed. Long story short: "You just needed to get your foot in the door."

***

What Do the Homeless Need?

It's time for some Major League Baseball tonight as the St. Louis Cardinals are hosting the Chicago Cubs! Before the game, you plan on meeting a couple of friends for drinks.

Since you're early and don't feel like paying $30 for parking, you decide to park a half-mile away from the stadium.

As you're walking to the restaurant, a homeless person (Jake) starts walking next to you. As you say, "Hello," he immediately asks for money right away. Not knowing what Jake will use the money for, you say, "Thank you for asking, but I will not give money today."

You notice that Jake is looking thin and that you're in no rush to meet your friends. Which makes you want to help out and offer to buy him dinner, and he takes you up on this kind gesture. The small talk starts, it turns out Jake use to be a cook, and recently he had a tough breakup with his girlfriend.

Connected to the stadium is the sports bar, where you decide to buy him food. There is no cover charge to enter, but since it's connected to the baseball stadium, there is a security line to go through. As you go through, you're surprised when Jake empties his pockets to see that there is **no cell phone**, **no wallet**, **no ID**, and **no cigarettes**. All that comes out of Jake's pockets are two run-down, battle-tested gas station lighters.

Since you're in public and Jake seems nice, this doesn't feel uncomfortable, but you have no idea what to expect.

The two of you find a spot at the bar and talk longer than expected. Jake sips through five glasses of ice-cold Coca-Cola, and you can see how grateful he is for this favor.

During your time together, it becomes apparent Jake's niche is cooking. He can cook all sorts of dishes like Chicken Parmesan, the "best" Chicken Wings in the world, and some fantastic Fettuccine Alfredo, to name a few.

Trying to help Jake in the long term and think the big picture you ask,

"How cool would it be to feed this whole place someday? To be able to give back? To be able to help people who have been in your shoes?"

Jake pauses for a second and takes a moment to think about what you said, and you follow up by saying,

"Look around at this restaurant."

[Pause]

"How fulfilling would it be to feed all of these people someday?"

[He smiles.]

"How nice would that be?"

[A long pause]

Finally, he says,

"Yeah, that would be pretty cool."

You can't tell how he interpreted what you said. But think…

Did it hit him hard? Did it go in one ear and out the other? Does he believe it is possible?

*

After making a tremendous effort to help Jake out, you give him a handshake and wish the best. At that moment, Jake leans in and whispers something to you, "Hey, you know it is going to be tough out there for me. Can you give me some money to walk away with?"

You are a little thrown off and a bit surprised as you've given him an hour of your time, free dinner, and a plan for him to get back on his feet.

Politely you say "No" and wish him the best.

*

Meeting with your friends afterward feels different because you can't seem to get what Jake told you off of your mind.

Why did he ask me for more money? When I gave him time, energy, and food.

Whatever the answer may be you showed you cared, you showed an open-mind, and you took a chance at positively impacting his life.

You gave him a chance to **think bigger** (even if it was just for a second), to **think differently** (even if it was just for a minute), and to **have a true friend** (even if it was just for an hour).

The truth is, giving him money will make him want to ask for more instead of going to earn it.

The truth is, giving him money will get him thinking more and more about the things that have got him there in the first place, and likely not go to good use.

The truth is that giving him money will not help him change his habits, it will not help him change his mindset, and it will not help him build a support team to get back to where he needs and wants to be.

*

What if we spent more time helping the homeless out? Instead of giving money to a person or place where we don't know where it's going.

What if we provided more places for them to turn things around, develop positive habits, and go after what it is they want?

What if we genuinely lent a hand to help the homeless?

What if, on top of donating food, we cooked a meal with

them, and then sat down and ate it with them as many families and friends do?

What if, on top of getting them pairs of shoes, we went on walks with them and listened to what they had on their minds?

What if, instead of giving money to them, we take them to the book store and have them pick out a couple of books that interested them?

What if on top of saying "Hi," we smile and compliment them or crack a joke?

*

What if homeless people just simply need…

HUMAN KINDNESS.

***

To Receive, You Have to Be Ready to Accept What Is Given

Compliments often bring this situation to life. Genuine compliments can make someone's day, attract someone into our life, and put smiles on faces. The opposite is also true: False or fake compliments are one of the easiest ways to decrease engagement and interest in conversations.

Three ways to ensure your compliments are ready to be received are:

(1) Add value to the person receiving the compliment. Something as simple as smiling or being present in a conversation can make the other person ready to

accept your praise.

(2) Mean what you are saying! People will know if you're BS-ing, they may call you out immediately or find out later what you said was fake. Either way, it won't work out well for you.

(3) Be able to explain what you meant by the compliment, if you say, "Hey! I like your shirt." You should be able to say why you like the shirt.

When giving a compliment, think:

- Are you giving this person enough value to want to receive it?
- Do you genuinely mean what you're saying?
- Can you explain the compliment in further detail?

***

Refining What Is Necessary for Improvement

"Absorb what is useful, Discard what is not, Add what is uniquely your own." – Bruce Lee

You've been working for a social media startup for a couple of years and have seen limited growth. Realizing it's tough to grow with this company and time for a change, you decide to start looking into working for a company at the top of the social media industry.

After spending weeks applying and interviewing, an opportunity arises. The company hiring you has over a hundred people on staff and an incoming class of twelve new employees.

Stepping into the office on your first day feels intimidating, competitive, and motivating. Since you're coming in with an average level of experience, you have no idea what to expect from the others.

The company hires one set of new employees a year to save time and ensure proper training. The orientation sessions are full of intensity, motivation, and commanding messages.

During the meeting, your boss glared across the room as if she had twenty-four eyes staring down at each individual in the area before saying,

"This business is only as strong as the weakest link. Everyone's thoughts and opinions are valued. Listen to what others have to say and refine what is necessary for improvement.

"Absorb what is useful, let go of what's not, and use what is already working for you to help yourself and the company grow.

"Through a team culture, we can accelerate growth.

"Michael Jordan didn't start winning championships until Phil Jackson convinced him...

"Good teams become great ones when the members trust each other enough to surrender the Me for the We.

"We will work together, refine what is necessary, and continue to grow as a team."

After this statement, out of everyone in the room, she looks directly at you and asks, "Make sense?" Sitting, staring, and shocked, you silently nod your head up and down.

For the first time, you've had clear expectations set on the first day, and you can now see why this company has had success up until this point.

***

Stepping Up to Buy the Family Business

You're a young female of twenty-eight. Up until this point, you've had a successful start to your career, having made over $80,000 a year, gotten two promotions, and you have a boss that appreciates your work ethic.

Inside, you're not happy though, because the finance industry hasn't given you the joy you thought it would.

One night you get a call from your stepmother who sounds like she could use a bucket for the tears coming out of her eyes. It turns out the family business is struggling.

For years, your family has run the top gym in town. Grampa started running the show forty years ago, and your dad and step-mother took over the past five years after he decided to step down.

Unfortunately, Dad's passion was in the money and not with the people in the gym, which led to poor service and business slowly trending downward.

During the high school years, you worked for your grandfather and had good memories. Leading to a tough decision:

Do you quit your job, move home, and help your parents turn things around?

Or

Do you let the gym slide and continue with a job that treats you well, even though you don't like it?

*

Making a gut decision, you decide to quit your job and start helping your family out. The transition to dealing with customer complaints, work orders, and a staff of employees are tough at first.

But after a couple of weeks go by, it's clear you're the go-to person at the gym for the staff and members, which leads you to officially becoming the general manager.

The gym is run better now, but dealing with the daily family mess is taking its toll on you. To end the madness, you decide to start looking into buying the business. The problem is, you have no business experience, leading to you enrolling in a fitness business seminar with your family.

During one of the seminar breaks, you ask for advice from the presenter. The presenter helps out, says what the family needed to hear, and explains how you can buy the business from your parents and keep everyone happy.

After this talk, your dad admits he wants to sell the business and is glad you're interested.

By staying open-minded, reaching out for help, and taking a chance, you were able to figure things out and keep everyone happy.

Unforgettable Experience

The Concert You Will Never Forget

There's a lot of excitement going on this afternoon because you're going to see Luke Bryan tonight! You're all dressed up, the pre-game festivities are in the truck, and you're only thirty minutes away from having the time of your life.

As you arrive, there are signs for parking, passenger drop-offs, and special vehicles. Even though the concert is sold out, there is hardly a wait to find a parking spot. The cars are flowing into spots that are perfectly organized by the parking attendants.

The lines for security are long, but moving fast. Within five minutes, you're through the gate and greeted by the staff with a company-sponsored camouflage koozie!

Having had a good time pregaming, your first stop in the venue is a trip to the restroom. As you walk in, you can't help noticing how clean it is. Two high school kids are helping keep the bathrooms up to standards with disinfectant spray in one hand and paper towels in the other. Not only are they keeping the place fresh, but they look like they're happy to be there, making your experience at the venue enjoyable.

Thanks to the signs and customer service, you're seats are easy to find. The attendant even walked you to your section.

The sound quality is excellent, and the warmup band sets the tone for the night, bringing energy and great music!

After the warmup band exits, grabbing a bite to eat seems like a solid play to help slow down your buzz from the alcohol. As you order, the person working the register says,

"Welcome to (fill in the blank) amphitheater, how may I help you?"

With a smile on your face, you order the buttered-down popcorn and send it straight into your mouth, as you are walking away from the register, you see someone sweeping up popcorn around the food area. After attending concerts at over thirty venues, you start to realize this may be the best one, best customer service, and the best experience you've ever had.

What else could they do to top this experience?

Intermission is brief after the opening band, it's twenty minutes and gives you enough time to use the restroom, grab a drink, and get ready for Luke! He performs for two-hours that night, sounding great, getting the crowd involved, and taking the stress off of your mind. You and your friends are on cloud nine, time flies by, and you know you won't have a voice in the morning from screaming and singing all night.

The concert may have been too much fun because your friend who drove probably had one too many drinks. On the stumbling walk out of the stadium, there's a black tent that wasn't there when you walked in. The tent says, "Police," and they are offering free breathalyzer tests. Perfect! To be safe, your friend who is driving blows into the breathalyzer and blows a .09. The cop recommends your friend doesn't drive home and explains how you can pick up the car tomorrow morning, and that there will be no tickets or tows until 2 PM the next day. He explains where the passenger pick-up is, and you'll take a rideshare back home, and everyone gets home safe.

*

As you reflect on the concert, it becomes apparent this experience was unforgettable. The next day, you are already looking up shows to attend at this venue.

This venue created opportunities for patrons to enjoy their time at the concert, had a safe and friendly environment, and provided an unforgettable experience that leaves customers dying to come back.

*

Details, customer service, and execution were the critical components for this experience. These are key factors that separate winners from losers, thriving businesses from failing ones, and **unforgettable experiences** from **never coming back**.

What is an unforgettable experience that you've had?

_____

_____

What made it unforgettable? What was done well?

_____

_____

What made the experience different from the others?

_____

_____

***

The Best Hosts Make You Feel Comfortable and
Leave You Wanting to Come Back

Being homesick seems to be a common thought throughout your first year at college. The real world isn't coming easy, as you find yourself scrambling up loose change for ramen noodles, loading up on food from Walmart when you receive your paycheck, and looking at an empty wallet/purse has become very frustrating!

Your friend's hometown is only forty-five minutes away from school, and his parents invited a handful of you over for dinner. His parents have been in your shoes before and know young adults away from home, sometimes could really use a home-cooked meal.

*

During the road trip up to your friend's house, it's nice to see what life's like away from college. There are houses, farmland, golf courses, malls, and it's much different than the college you've been in the last couple of months.

As you pull into your friend's house, it passes the eye test immediately. It is nice in size, has a long driveway, followed by a substantial backyard, and a happy couple welcoming you at the door.

WOW! What a first impression.

His parents give you a tour of the house, and what stands out the most is the office. There is a massive library of books, with a wide variety of genres that are all organized alphabetically.

You ask your friend's Mom why they have this library. She says, "We have this library of books because there are two ways you can learn…

    1.) From your mistakes

    Or

    2.) From other people's mistakes

"… not only do books make you smarter, but they are buckets of information authors put together to help people learn quicker."

You've never looked at reading as fun because of always being forced to read books of no interest to you. But now you have a reason to read. If there is something you want to learn, you find a book and learn from the author's mistakes.

*

Dinner that night is heavenly - there are steaks, mashed potatoes, green vegetables, warm bread, all cooked and seasoned to perfection. The meal is so good; you start to wonder if this is what heaven is like!

The conversations at dinner are engaging and enjoyable. There is an air of gratitude, and you can tell the family cares about everyone at the table. Dessert is served, and why not enjoy it? The savory taste of the pumpkin pie settles into your mouth, and life is good!

After the dinner ends, you begin to realize this family is successful in multiple aspects of life. You ask your friend's dad, "What does it take to be successful?"

He says, "It's simple. How you do anything is how you do everything. If you want to be successful, treat everything you do like a successful person would.

"Be the best greeter at the house, at work, and to strangers.

"Take care of your house and car, like you would your job.

"Clean the dishes like it's a million-dollar deal.

"If a crumb falls on the ground, pick it up as if it were $100.

"If you're going to do something, do it right. That's it."

It starts coming together now, as this family gave you and your friends an unforgettable experience. But it wasn't just for you. That's how they do everything.

**

Handling Fears Through Superior Service

Having to travel for work this week on short notice leaves you with no choice but to book an Airbnb. With an Airbnb, you don't always know what you're getting into, but there are two things you'd like to see.

First, you want it to be safe. Second, you want to feel welcome and taken care of. These two concepts help to handle fears and help generate repeat customers.

*

Before walking into the Airbnb, there is a message from the host with step-by-step directions for everything.

A code for the entrance, pictures of the room you're staying in, and a key waiting for you. Right away, it feels better than staying at a hotel.

*

Having had a couple of drinks at the social that night, you want water before bed to make sure you're ready for tomorrow. As you walk into your room, just past your bed, you see two bottles of water sitting there for you. It's almost like they read your mind!

There are also a fresh set of towels and a paper posted containing all the house rules, the Wi-Fi password, and more.

Walking into the bathroom, you see shampoo, body wash, and face towels ready for you.

Making you feel welcomed, safe, and confident towards keeping your focus on work this week.

*

In the morning, you discover a community fridge and freezer stocked with breakfast goods: Eggs, frozen berries, oatmeal, bread, and packages of different nut butter.

*

A stress-free and filling breakfast leads to a successful meeting that day and after you tell your co-workers about your Airbnb experience.

By handling fears through superior service, this Airbnb made you feel welcome and taken care of, which are keys to creating an unforgettable experience, increased referrals, and re-occurring customers.

***

Reversing the Bad Day

Orlando is the destination for your next business trip. On the plane ride down, you have the pleasure of sitting next to a mother and her sugar-high five-year-old.

Shortly after the plane takes off, the five-year old's sugar high hits a wall, and he pukes all over your leg! You jump up and manage to dodge the puke, but your face can't dodge the overhead bins, and you end up with a shiny red mark the size of a golf ball.

Your long day gets longer when your driver to the hotel can't find you. Twenty-five minutes later, he arrives. Not helping the delay, the driver doesn't speak your language and takes five wrong turns on the way.

As you step out of the car, the curb catches your foot unexpectedly, and you stagger straight into a puddle of water, where your phone slips out of your hand onto the sidewalk. The phone survives the fall, but your right leg is soaking wet, covered in puddle water.

The hotel receptionist can tell you've had a rough day and asks if everything is okay.

You respond by saying, "It has been a rough day." That was all she needed to hear before saying,

"I understand today has been a rough day. Take your time getting settled into your room, and when you come back down, we will have dinner and a glass of wine waiting for you. On us!"

After a shower and change of clothes, you come down to the restaurant. The hostess has a smile on her face and walks you to a table. Within five minutes, you're enjoying a wonderful steak dinner, paired with the best tasting red wine ever.

One of the worst days you've ever had has now turned into one of the best.

What a day!

*

The hotel looked at this situation as an opportunity to help a guest out. They gave up direct revenue from the meal, but will likely have a loyal customer for life

***

Service Is Always Senior to Selling

It's time to start your first "real" job. You're excited because with every sale you make a 2% commission. The problem is you don't know how to sell!

It's safe to say your confidence is not high right now, as you've only made one sale in the last two weeks, which makes you want to learn the people who are making sales.

After observing, it becomes apparent that Jane is the best at sales in the department and she makes sale, after sale, after sale. Finally, building up enough courage to ask Jane for help, you ask her if she'd like to get lunch this week. At lunch, the conversation goes,

"How do you do it? I've been trying hard to sell the products and have had no luck."

She explains: "Service is always senior to selling someone. Everything from the introduction to handling objections, to assisting based on their needs, to elevating your service above and beyond is what's necessary to sell."

You thank Jane for her time and think about providing service, instead of trying to sell.

*

The next day you show up to work, ask customers how you can help, and answer any questions they have. As a result, you double the sales of your first two weeks in a single day! As you made two entire sales.

SERVICE>>>>SELLING

ACTIVE LIFESTYLE

It's Your Duty to Take Care of Yourself

It's a big week...

- You have a presentation on Wednesday in front of a dozen board members, and your CEO will also be there.
- On Friday night, you have the first "real" date with someone you like.
- Then you're going to a family reunion all day Saturday.

*

On Monday night, you feel a sore throat is near. The big week is here, and it's the worst time to be coming down with a cold! At this point, all you can think about is getting rid of it and feeling better.

The voice inside your head says, "Why does this have to come now, why to me?"

*

At this moment, all you want to do is get well and focus on your health. But on Sunday the opposite was true as you stayed up until 2 AM eating popcorn and chugging Red Bulls.

Why is this?

When we're young, we often take advantage of our health to work on our wealth. But when we put on excess weight, get completely out of shape, or find ourselves getting sick at the worst times! We tend to regret not taking better care of our health, which leads us to spend our wealth on our health through medications, doctors' bills, personal trainers, physical therapists, diet plans, etc.

*

There's a famous quote, "If you have your health, you have hope. If you have hope you have everything."

It is your obligation to take care of yourself. For you, your family, your job, your loved ones, and the people around you.

Taking care of your health allows you to work on your wealth and take care of the people closest to you. Which, in return, gives you increased chances to do what you want, when you want, with the people you want.

Hope gives you what's needed to make things happen. But it can also be paralyzing if a thought or idea doesn't get followed by an action. Without action, hope gives you just about nothing.

If you have your health, what will you do to take advantage of it and go after what you want?

_____

_____

_____

If you don't have your health where it needs to be, what can you do to search for answers, look for solutions, ask questions, and do everything you can to get back to where you want to be? If things happen, what will you do to fight back?

_____

_____

_____

If you have a chronic or fatal issue, fight to find answers for other people who may be in that same position. Look what Jimmy Valvano did. He had cancer that he knew was going to lead to his passing. He still fought and started a foundation that is helping others fight and survive twenty-five-plus years later.

Dr. Joe Dispenza is a great person to learn from if you have a condition that has been tough to diagnose, or that has been hard on you physically or mentally.

***

The More You Take Care of Your Body, The More It Will Take Care of You

Summertime is such a great time to be alive. The weather is nice, schools out, and vacations are near. One morning your friend invites you to the beach to hang out. But you're too ashamed to wear a swimsuit in front of people and make up an excuse why you won't be able to go.

After lying to your friend, you can't tell if you're motivated to lose weight or depressed from not being in the shape you want. But you do realize it's time to make a change.

To start, you go for a five-minute walk every day. Then you

start sprinkling in lite workouts at home. Looking for increased motivation and an extra push, you find yourself in a group training class four days a week. Throughout the process, one of the trainers mentioned eating to 80% full and making whole foods the majority of your daily consumption to help lose weight.

Before you know it, it's the end of the summer, and twenty pounds are gone. You feel good, look great, and are hanging out at the beach with your friends. You made positive changes to take care of your body through workouts and nutrition, and your body responded by giving you what you've been searching for.

***

Phones Are Life, or Are They?

If you didn't have a phone for a week, what would you do?

Would you buy a notebook and write?

Would you grab a paintbrush and paint?

Would you go outside for a walk with a friend?

Would you introduce yourself to people you've never met before?

Would you spend more time moving around, instead of scrolling through social media?

Would you enjoy it?

Would you be less stressed and more motivated?

Would you be relieved to not listen for a "buzz-buzz" or a

vibration feeling in your pocket?

*

What would life be like without phones? How much would face-to-face communication improve?

What are 5-10 things you'd do if you didn't have a phone for a week?

1.) _____
_____
2.) _____
_____
3.) _____
_____
4.) _____
_____
5.) _____
_____

<u>Positivity</u>

Bringing Value to Someone as You Cross Paths

It's sunny and seventy-five degrees with a nice breeze and a great day to be on vacation. It's a perfect morning for a walk on the beach. On your hour walk, they are nice views, ocean waves, and soft sand. During this time, you cross paths with a lady walking by. She smiles at you and doesn't say a word. Without saying a word, she just made your day because of this simple act of human kindness.

*

Moments later, as you walk by another woman. She looks down at her phone and completely ignores you. With no words exchanged, you wonder why it is so hard to say hello and acknowledge that I'm here.

*

The point here is simple: Bringing value to someone can be as easy as smiling while you walk by each other.

What is one act of human kindness you will do today to bring value to someone? (Ex. Smile, Say Hello, Give a compliment)

_____

_____

***

The Swear Word That Changed Your Life

It's another day working at the store. Customers in, customers out. It has become routine to say, "How are you?" "Have a good day," and "Thank you for shopping with us."

On the flip side, it seems routine to hear back "Doing good" and "Thanks, you too."

*

One day a customer comes in, smiles at you, and tells you their day is going great before you can say, "Thank you for coming in." As the customer leaves, he looks you in the eyes and says, "Hope you have a kick-ass rest of your day."

Your vibe completely changes. Your outlook on your job is now positive, the crap you don't want to do when you get home is off your mind, and the rest of your day has turned into something worth looking forward to.

Why is this?

It's because positivity spreads, just like negativity does. With excitement, energy, and passion, good vibes can be attracted.

*

Now, you know it's possible to make someone's day by switching things up. You start saying "great" instead of "good," you begin smiling instead of nodding your head, and you start to express words with passion and positive emotion.

Three weeks go by, and your boss seems to notice this change and decides you're ready for a promotion. He explains that you seem to be a different person, how you have different energy (in the right way), and that you have had many compliments from the customers lately.

Sometimes positivity, passion, and excitement can be the easiest way to get a raise or promotion.

***

Negative People Are Not Fun

Positivity attracts Positive People.

Negativity attracts Negative People.

Which type of person would you like to attract to your life? Why?

_____
_____

What is one thing you will do to be more positive today?

_____
_____

Leading By Example

Wise Words from the Great Steven Covey

"Leadership is communicating to another person their worth and potential so clearly they are inspired to see it in themselves." – Steven Covey, *Primary Greatness*

Change isn't easy. Think back to a time you made a change. Did you do it for yourself, for someone else, or because you were forced to do so? Did you have guidance, help, and support?

Whether the change is for you, someone you genuinely care about, or an employee/co-worker working with you, it's essential to **lead by example**.

*

If you clean consistently, others will likely clean more often.

If you do not clean consistently, others will likely not clean, and you'll be less likely to have a job that wants you or roommates that will want to live with you.

*

If you want a loved one to stop smoking or to lose weight and you don't smoke, and you eat healthy foods, they will tend to shift toward those.

If you do smoke around them, eat fast food, and bug them about their diet, they will probably go back to their old ways.

What type of support system, leader, and friend will you be?

_____

_____

_____

***

Take Care of Yourself First, Before You Take Care of Others

While you're traveling by plane to San Diego, the flight attendants are going over the safety protocols. As they go over what to do when the oxygen mask comes down, they explain you should put your mask on before helping the person next to you.

Why is this?

It's because if you don't take care of yourself, how are you going to take care of the person next to you and other people after that?

Putting your mask on first gives you a chance to help others. If your mask never gets put on when the air quality gets out of control, you won't be able to help because you'll be dead or passed out.

*

If you don't lead by example, it is going to be tough to help other people out.

- If a trainer isn't in shape, why would you go to him/or her?
- If a dentist doesn't have good teeth, why would you go to him/or her?

- If a nutritionist is overweight, why would you go to him/or her?
- If a barber or hairdresser has terrible hair, why would you go to him/or her?
- If an interviewee has a wrinkled shirt during an interview, why would you hire him/or her?

*

The truth is…

If you don't take care of yourself, it will be tough to take care of others. And if you don't take care of others, you will likely struggle with growth at work, have trouble sustaining and growing relationships, and you will have to live with not being able to step up when needed.

Positively leading by example will work wonders.

***

You're in Control, What Are You Going to Do About It?

Situation 1: You're stuck at a meeting about fifteen minutes away from your house. The snow is coming down, and the winter storm warning says it's hitting big! They're saying 12–16 inches:

Do you take the risk and try to drive back home?

Or

Do you fork up extra money and stay at the hotel nearby?

*

Situation 2: You have to get to work early tomorrow and are grabbing a couple of drinks with your friends the night before. Time flies by, drinks get handed to you, and you've met an awesome group of people you're hitting it off with. After glaring over at the clock by the bar that reads "1 AM," you realize it's time to head back home!

Even though you're probably over the limit, you tell your friends you're good to drive. You think…

Do I take the risk and drive back home?

Or

Do I take a car service back and pay the extra $15?

*

Many of us have been in at least one of these situations. What should you do? What have you chosen to do in the past? What will you do in the future?

*

We often know what we should do, but why do we often find ourselves questioning it?

Is it because a DWI costs $7,000+ and a lot of stress? Is it because if you drive intoxicated, not only will you be risking your life, your car's value, but the lives of others? Is it because you would not be in control?

If you're not in control, bad things can happen: The car can slide off the road, you can blackout and run into a tree, and of course, you can get a DUI.

The point being: If you're not in control, is it worth it?

*

In life, you have control. You have the freedom to make decisions, not only about driving but with the actions you take. Take a second to think about the following…

What type of car do you want?

Cool, work for it.

What type of house do you want?

Cool, work for it.

What type of job do you want?

Cool, go get it.

What type of husband or wife do you want?

Excellent, go find him or her and work to attract your future significant other into your life.

What type of mother or father do you want to be?

Great, lead by example, and be that person.

*

You decide to attract what you want into your life. If you aren't getting what you want, find ways to attract what you want. Push yourself to do bigger, better, and greater things.

During your time on Earth, you have control of what you can and will accomplish. What are you going to do about that?

Are you going to come up with excuses consistently?

Or

Are you going to work hard to accomplish something special?

***

Small Daily Wins Add Up to Big Wins Over Time

Would you rather win or lose?

If you said win, I agree it feels incredible and losing feels awful.

When you hear the names of Tom Brady and Michael Jordan, what is the first thought that comes to mind?

A winner, right?

What do you think of when hearing the words failing, unsuccessful, negative, poor?

Probably not great thoughts, right?

Is this because these are words that aren't associated with fun, that most people wouldn't want in their life, or that these words feel like losing?

Losing isn't always bad because the more losses you get may lead to more wins if appropriate action is taken.

But would you agree that winning feels better?

Of course, it does. Winning is one of the greatest highs in life, and the formula for it is simple.

Winners are consistent, winners hold themselves accountable, or find someone to hold them responsible, and winners take action!

Do you have a system to help you win? That keeps you consistently learning and growing?

If yes, great; how is that working for you? If no, give this a thought…

What if you played a game every day where you either won the day or lost the day? With this daily game, you're consistently challenged to be better, to do more, and to achieve great things. What if this game had daily tasks that needed to be accomplished to get a win? But not just everyday tasks, critical tasks to push you toward your goals. And what if your critical tasks led to positive habits over time? Do you think that, by consistently challenging yourself, you'd grow? You'd learn? You'd provide a path for yourself to succeed?

Think about this…

When writing a book, it's understandable not to know how to start. After drawing blanks for days, you start writing about something enjoyable and eventually come up with chapter titles. With the chapter titles, ideas blossom to help complete the rough draft, which leads to getting the book edited. After putting its finishing touches on, it gets published!

If you took one step every day to finish the book, the book

would likely get done. If you started, stopped, and second-guessed yourself, chances are the necessary work wouldn't get done.

It's crucial to find a system that holds you accountable, that breeds consistency, and that keeps you moving toward your goals.

You will not win every day, but if you win twenty-five out thirty days in a month, would you agree that it is a pretty good record?

What are the five critical tasks you can do tomorrow?

1.) _____

_____

2.) _____

_____

3.) _____

_____

4.) _____

_____

5.) _____

_____

*At the end of the day, check off all of the tasks you did. If you have a checkmark next to all of the tasks, then write "WIN" next to the day. If you can't complete all of the tasks, mark it as a loss and move the tasks that were incomplete from the previous day on to the next day.

***

Berardi's First Law

"If a food is in your house or possession, either you, someone you love, or someone you marginally tolerate, will eventually eat it." – John Berardi

"If a healthy food is in your house or possession, either you, someone you love, or someone you marginally tolerate, will eventually eat it." – John Berardi

John Berardi of Precision Nutrition came up with this law, which means if you have healthy food around, then you and the people around you will likely eat healthily.

If you have unhealthy food around, then you and the people around will likely eat unhealthily.

*

If you want someone to lose weight, then **lead by example** and help the person you care about by having healthy food around.

It's that simple.

How often has telling someone…

"Hey, you shouldn't eat that."

"_____ needs to lose weight."

"This is what you need to eat."

"This is what you need to avoid eating."

"This is the diet you need to be on. It will get you the results you are looking for."

…worked for you or the people you care about in the past?

Leading by example starts a process of wanted action versus forced action.

Please think about this before trying to force someone to change.

What can you do to lead by example to help someone change? Your answer does not have to be nutrition-related.

_____
_____
_____

Consistency

Ten Concepts Towards Consistency and Fulfillment

1) Know Your Numbers

How much money does it cost for you to survive?

How much money did you spend last year?

Last month?

How much money are you trying to make in the future? Next year? Next month?

*

Ask any successful business owner: What is the leading cause of failed businesses'? Many would say not knowing their numbers.

Your life is a business. If you don't have target numbers to hit, what's going to push you through the late nights when all you want to do is pull your hair out and quit?

How are you going to know if it was a good month financially or a bad month?

Numbers push you to do more, know more, and achieve more.

One way to track numbers is to record your cash transactions on the notes on your phone. Then at the end of the month, figure out how much you spent with credit card(s) and checks.

After that is done, add the cash, check, and credit card transactions up.

Now you know how much you spent last month. Subtract this from what you made after taxes, and that is your profit or loss for the month.

Once you know your numbers, you can come up with a goal to shoot for each month and try to beat.

Remember, your life is a business! Knowing your numbers will help refine your financial future.

2)   What the Greats Do Well to Develop Wealth

If you could have one superpower, what would it be?

_____

_____

*

Bill Gates and Warren Buffet got asked that question, and they said their one superpower would be to read faster.

Why do you think this is?

It's because they know the answers are out there, but that they may have to search for them.

In a book, an author condenses a lifetime worth of knowledge and gives the reader added experience, education, and practical application to help learn faster.

You can learn from your mistakes, or you can learn from other people's mistakes. Make time to learn wisely.

3) Find Ways to Stay Active That You Enjoy

You only have one life – how should you treat your body?

Will you take care of it and let it take care of you?

Will you stay inactive and not let it take care of you?

It sounds like an easy decision, but it's ultimately up to you!

*

Here's a situation to think about:

You get challenged to do one-hundred pull-ups today. The problem is you can only do TWO!

What are you going to do?

What if you did one pull-up every sixty seconds, and when you were tired, you put a band around your foot to help assist you up. You may be tired, and they may not look like traditional pull-ups, but by the end of the day, you've done one-hundred pull-ups.

What if you used your time and resources for your

health? How much knowledge would you have gained?

What type of shape would you be in?

*

It's often asked, "How often should I work out?"

The answer is, it depends. But the real answer is the rest of your life. Working out is a lifestyle. It's what our bodies need to stay strong, moving well, and coordinated.

How you do this could vary from the gym to dancing, to yard work, to tasks or games at home with family and friends.

Remember, the more you take care of your body, the more it takes care of you.

4) Fueling Your Body Properly

What you put in your body directly correlates to how effective your energy levels are along with the function of your immune system.

With that said, would you agree that it's essential to know what foods work well for you and which foods don't?

No one wants to get sick the day before a big date, a big test, a big tournament, a family reunion, an audition.

If you don't prepare, life can take unwanted turns.

Is this a broad statement, yes. But it's here to make you think about ways to prepare your body better. Cooking meals ahead of time is a way to help prepare better. In the end, it saves time, and you know what's in the food.

Think about the following questions:

What foods do you like?

What foods make you feel good?

What food gives you sustained energy? If you don't know what does – what foods can you experiment with?

How and when will you make time to prepare your food?

When will you get groceries? Where will you get them from?

These are all things to consider when working on finding the best ways to prepare your body to run and function the way it's needed to make great things happen.

The "how-to" nutrition answers won't be given here because this book is designed to get you thinking about what needs to be executed on in your life.

Precision Nutrition is a great company to check out if you want to learn about how to fuel your body correctly, cook new things, and attain/maintain healthy habits.

5) Working on Yourself to Be a Better Future Boyfriend, Girlfriend, Husband, Wife

Whether you're in a relationship or not, if you desire to be in one or to make your current one the best one possible, what are you doing to work on it?

If you are not in a relationship, what are you doing to be a better future boyfriend/girlfriend?

Are you defining what you're looking for? Are you learning from other relationships you respect and admire? Are you working on yourself to be in great shape and to grow your wealth? Are you getting a better understanding of peoples love languages? Are you discovering the necessary traits you need to attract the person you're looking for in your life?

*

If you're in a relationship, what are you doing to bring value and spark your relationship consistently?

Do you know your significant others, love language(s)?

Do you spend enough quality time with him or her?

Do you perform random acts of service for your significant other? Such as bringing flowers or writing a handwritten card on a random day to express your love. Or even simple tasks around the house, such as taking out the trash and doing the dishes without being asked?

Do you give the right gifts? Whether it's a nice watch or a glowing necklace. Or maybe that compass from their grandpa you dug deep to find at their parents' house. What is a meaningful gift to your significant other? Does it have to be expensive, thoughtful, or both?

Do you consistently affirm your loved one appropriately? By giving authentic compliments, telling them when they're right or wrong, and letting him or her know you can be trusted by expressing this in ways where you never say the word "trust."

Do you consistently express the physical touch necessary to keep your loved one happy? Do you have enough romance to satisfy his/or her needs, do you give a hug when needed, do you hold his/or her hand when it's asking to be held onto?

Whether you're in a relationship or not…

By taking action, by finding out people's needs and wants, and by consistently refining this process, you're setting yourself up for a kick-ass future relationship or a current one that keeps growing.

6)   Grandparents Are Full of Experiences

Who's been through more than your grandparents?

If they have passed away, what would they say to you right now if they were here? If it's impossible to think of this, try spending a couple of hours talking to the elderly at an assisted living home.

What did you notice? What did they say? What was it like? Did they have regrets? Did they have good or bad memories to share? Did they give you advice?

As stated earlier, there are two ways to learn in life:

From your own mistakes or other people's mistakes. I mentioned at the beginning of the book that, from working in an assisted living home in high school, I became aware that some people lived life up and were happier than can be, some talked about their loved ones (especially grandkids), while others expressed regret, some even constantly had the look of regret on their faces which was tough to see.

What better people to learn from, than the ones who have seen it all? Grandparents and elders may care more than most because, when you can't do as much as you used to, sometimes loved ones are the ones you think about the most. Loved ones can make their day, keep hopes up, stress them out, cause worry, and make them happy.

What's something you can do to give back to the elderly?

_____

_____

Whether they are family or not, they are people who have lived lives full of knowledge and experiences. They still want to have fun, and they still want to look forward to things, they still have time – and so do you.

What will you do to make the most out of your time left on this planet?

_____

_____

7) You Are the Average of the People You Surround Yourself With

When you think of growing up, your parents/guardians are likely the first people who come to mind.

You may remember those fresh pies mom used to bake on Thanksgiving, playing catch in the backyard with your dad, or even the time when your parents drove you to Disney World.

The tough times may also may come to mind, like the fights between parents that kept you up at night, that constant smell of smoke or cite of cigarettes, or that time when no one showed up to your game or competition.

Either way, the people who raised you have had a significant influence on your life, whether it was for better or for worse. Why is this? It's because people tend to act and be like the people they hang around with the most. Some may agree, some may disagree. But the people you surround yourself with have a significant impact on your life experiences and ultimately how you will live your life.

Who will you spend your time with, and why with them?

List five people you'd like to spend more time with:

1.) _____
2.) _____
3.) _____
4.) _____
5.) _____

8) What Is True Happiness?

Whether it's for the good or bad, "happiness' is a word we often hear in today's society. The dictionary might say happiness is feeling pleasure or content. However, because it's a feeling, it's tough to measure.

Would you agree with me that true happiness is doing what you want, when you want, with the people you want?

Imagine for a second hanging out with good friends, enjoying a glass of wine to the closing sunset. Or, picture yourself climbing that mountain on your bucket list. What if tomorrow, you knew you could wake up without an alarm clock because you had enough passive income to work on your terms? How would that feel?

What's one thing that makes you happy?

_____
_____

What is one thing that needs to change to make sure you do more stuff, as you mentioned above?

_____

_____

When are you going to make time for your happiness?

_____

_____

9) Quality Traits of a Good Friend

You're trying to figure out what a true friend is and what character traits he or she should portray.

What does a good friend represent to you? Write down five to ten traits.

_____

_____

_____

_____

_____

_____

_____

_____

Should a good friend be present when you talk to them?

- By staying off their phone and giving you the attention necessary for a quality chat
- By being there to lend a hand when you've had a tough day

- By looking at you in the eye while being authentically engaged in the conversation

Should a good friend communicate clearly?

- By being straight-forward
- By filling you in with appropriate things in their life
- By expressing words of affirmation

Should a good friend take initiative?

- By following through on acts of service
- By remembering your birthday and sending a card
- By adjusting their mood based on how you are feeling that day

Should a good friend make time to listen to you?

- By being understanding
- By staying up with you until five in the morning on "one of those nights"
- By rephrasing things you are saying to be engaged in the conversation

Should a good friend be loyal?

- By following through on promises
- By not talking behind your back
- By giving honest feedback

Should a good friend make time instead of making excuses?

- By driving an hour out of the way to take you to the airport when you couldn't find a ride
- By being there when you need a friend
- By consistently doing things to improve and positively influence the friendship

Should a good friend be positive?

- By holding you up when you fall down
- By cutting out negativity because negative people suck
- By making you feel better instead of worse

Should a good friend show they care?

- By speaking your love language (Quality Time, Words of Affirmation, Gifts, Acts of Service, or Physical Touch)
- By asking how your day was and engaging with a caring nature
- By consistently finding and showing he or she cares in a variety of ways

Should a good friend bring value to the friendship?

- By helping you do the right thing instead of making a poor decision
- By making you a better person
- By allowing you to have fun and enjoy the time you spend together

What is a good friend to you?

_____

_____

_____

10) Commitment Is the Foundation of Great Accomplishments

Without commitment, are accomplishments possible?

Commitment starts a process of finding a way and paving a path toward your desires.

Commitment allows you to stay focused through the long hours, failed attempts, ups and downs, and helps push you through the tough times. The hard work and consistency throughout the process are what make these accomplishments feel great.

*

With wins over time, refining your desires, and consistency, you can accomplish great things.

What are you willing to commit to?

With your health?

1.) _____

2.) _____

3.) _____

4.) _____

With your wealth?

1.) _____

2.) _____

3.) _____

4.) _____

With your relationships?

1.) _____
2.) _____
3.) _____
4.) _____

With your happiness?

1.) _____
2.) _____
3.) _____
4.) _____

Write down four for each, refine for as long as needed, and commit!

<u>RESPECT</u>

A Lesson Learned From Partying

It's your junior year of college; you're enjoying the freedom of being on your own and the good times with your friends.

*

Throughout college, you've decided to make time to work out consistently. By your junior year, you started to know what you were doing in the gym, and people started working out with you.

Not thinking much of it, you keep designing workouts for you and a couple of friends. Before you know it, a half dozen people are working out with you. Realizing these students could use you as a coach/trainer, you split them up into two different time slots and give them your full attention throughout their workout. Even though you're training your friends for free, respect is starting to be earned from your peers, which has created an opportunity for yourself to become a better trainer.

*

That same year you decided to get a party house with a couple of your close friends and have been having a blast on the weekends. You'll agree to be welcoming and let people come to your house as long as they respect you.

Before you know it, fifty-to-sixty people are coming to your house every weekend. It turns out to be a great marketing opportunity for you, as people get to know you and the word spreads that you're the gym expert.

These parties allow you to have fun and enjoy life, as well as improve your network of people, which helped lead you to work on **selling** why people should workout with you and the **communication skills** necessary to attract new clients

At the parties, you start to notice most people who say they will come to see you in the gym next week don't show up. But the word keeps spreading that you are the go-to fitness expert.

*

After your junior year, you're ready to learn more and decide to do a fitness internship at the top gym in the world. You figure: If I'm going to pursue this passion, why not learn from the best?"

The internship involves long hours, minimal pay, and a tight living situation. What better way to learn at twenty-one years old! Your main takeaways from the internship include:

- People don't care how much you know until they know how much you care.
- Never teach something you haven't done.
- People feed off quality leadership.

*

As you get back to school for your senior year, many of the students show interest in working out with you. By the end of the year school year, about fifty students end up training with you. What a great way to start your career!

*

After graduation, you're ready to move on, and you get your first "big job" out of college.

Having had success with this job and finally making some real money, you decide it's time to go back to your school and speak on leadership because being a leader is your main role as a trainer.

You're excited to speak in front of many students who look up to you and want to learn about leadership.

*

After building your network of people in college through classes, parties, and training, you assume everyone will come and show support. The day of the presentation comes, and you bump into many of the students you were fortunate enough to meet throughout your time at school. Many of your close friends you use to party with are coming up to you throughout the day to say hello, and many students say something along the lines, "I can't wait to see you present today."

You're nervous, anxious, and excited about your presentation!

*

The presentation goes well, and the room was packed full. All is good, and you can't wait to celebrate with your buddies, just like the old times.

Later that night you meet up with your friends at a party and realize an important life lesson. None of the friends at the party that night were at your presentation.

What? Even with a crowded room, none of them were there?
Nope, you've realized almost everyone who came to see you speak was the people you impacted through training, being

authentic, and through referrals from people who knew you.

You start to realize...

- the people who respected you
- the people who cared enough to show up
- the people who looked up to you

Weren't the ones you partied with, but the ones you positively impacted.

*

The point of this story is to get readers thinking about impact and not that friends you party with don't have your back, because they absolutely can.

For example, instead of being disappointed that the friends you partied with didn't show up, you start working on being more compatible at parties and trying to bring value to your friends just like you do at the gym.

*

What's one step you can take today to become a better friend?

_____

_____

***

Why Give Up? You Might Be the Best Person for That

You're in a slump because your dream of opening up a retail clothing store is slowly slipping away. You've studied your competition, learned from various business owners through internships and management positions, and have been giving your all toward achieving this dream.

With the industry taking a turn away from community retail stores, you don't know what to do and find yourself talking it out with your cousin during Thanksgiving weekend.

*

Two years ago, you found yourself sitting at the beach.

Thinking…

Searching for answers…

Just trying to figure out where to go next in life…

*

Style, fashion, and clothing have always been something of interest to you. Thinking back to when you were a kid, you realized there wasn't anyone to teach you what to wear, what colors match, how to iron clothes properly, and what shoes to get.

So you start thinking about how to start a business to help young adults learn how to dress, how to take care of clothes, how to act like a professional, and where they can buy clothes from for an affordable price. The "all-in-one" store!

*

While attending a business conference later that year, you find the keynote speaker sitting at the bar. There's a moment for you to slip in and express your dream to him, just hoping he'll give you something to get you going in the right direction.

After expressing your dream to start the retail store for young adults, the speaker says, "Great, go buy or lease property and start a store." Like it was nothing! You start wondering if it's that simple.

The speaker knew it wasn't that simple. But, at the same time, this may have been the best advice someone could give you because he supported your dream.

You take his advice and start looking into what it takes to buy or lease property, own a store, and develop a team.

It turns out you have a long way to go and a lot to learn, which leads you into your first internship at a local tee-shirt shop. During this internship, you learn how to make custom shirts, hats, and coats on top of seeing how all of the orders are done. You also got plenty of hands-on experience in handling customer complaints and saw the ins and outs of wholesale pricing.

After six months of working twenty hours a week, you realize there is more to learn, specifically about professional fittings, style, and handling the upper class.

*

All this thought leads you to ask for a job at the local suit shop. Since you seem eager to help out, they agree to hire you at minimum wage, and your foot's in the door.

From working in their system and learning how to fit a suit

faster than anyone there, you receive a raise plus commission bonuses.

Only nine months after starting, you become the top fitter at the store and get promoted to manager. For the next nine months, you learn about leadership skills, profit and loss systems, organization, setting expectations, and, most important, you develop killer customer service skills.

*

After about two years of pursuing this dream, you find out the suit store is going out of business. As you dig deep into the details, it is easy to see why: Online custom fitting sites are taking over the retail industry, and there isn't much hope for your future dream!

*

That brings you back to Thanksgiving with your family, casually sitting in the living room when cousin asks you what you've been up to lately.

You haven't seen each other for a while, and it seems like any normal conversation as you start telling Cousin Jane about your dream, and how you're in a significant slump because of the store closing and the online custom fitting sites taking over.

Your cousin seems to be engaged in the conversation and to be listening thoroughly. After hearing you ramble on with depressing thoughts and complaints about how your dream got crushed, your cousin speaks up and says,

"Listen, there is always going to be a need for clothes and a place to buy them from.

"What if the clothing industry needs you? It does because you will be the best at portraying this message, your message.

"What if the industry needs you to set the standard for local retail clothing shops so that they can succeed?

"What if you are the best person for a local retail clothing shop?

"Why are you going to let one thing set you back when you could be letting a lot of people down if you do not pursue this dream?

"What if you are the answer to the 'hit-back' against the online stores?"

You now have a new breath of fresh air! This conversation came out of nowhere and left you feeling more motivated than ever.

*

Years later, you thank your cousin because you have just started your business. The store is up and running; not only are you selling clothes, but you're making a difference in the community.

You have specific nights to help young adults learn how to iron their clothes, prepare them for job interviews, look clean-cut, and help them act like true professionals.

Not only have you started a store, but you started a movement allowing young adults to learn important concepts that will benefit them the rest of their lives.

*

You now have a retail clothing store, the best custom fitting store around, and are a mentor to many young adults in the community.

Your cousin taught you an important life lesson that day, which has led you toward your dream and allowed you to leave a positive impact on the community. The world needs and wants more people like this…like you!

***

Learning from Power Couples Can Improve Your Relationships

It's hard to believe that only a few years ago, you were partying and enjoying college with your friends. Now you find yourself frequently traveling and working hard to make it. Before your flight back from a conference in Boston, you catch up with a college friend for breakfast who's been in a serious relationship for the past four years.

At this point in your life, dating, random hookups, and short flings aren't on your mind much compared to a long-term serious relationship, like the one your friend is in.

*

Breakfast is filled with great conversations and delicious food. One thing that jumps out to you is on their coffee table are two books.

Tom Brady's (*TB12 Method*) and Gisele Bundchen's (*Lessons: My Path to a Meaningful Life*).

When seeing this, some words come to mind…

Power Couple. Respect. Growth. Role Models. Success!

Impressed by this, you become involved in a conversation about the books. It turns out that Gisele and Tom are role models for most people in the Boston area.

Interested to hear what has been working well for this couple, you ask, "What do you attribute to the success of your relationship over the years?"

They answer by expressing how their values have been the keys to their success: Specifically, **respect** and **communication**.

*

In a relationship, respect has to work both ways; not only do you have to be respected by the other person, but it's important to show your respect back.

Different ways of doing this may be understanding that when we go through tough times, mood swings may happen. In these moments, being there for each other, actively listening, and giving a shoulder to lean on may be all that is needed. Sitting there and listening during rocky times can go a long way toward earning respect.

Compliments and authenticity can also go a long way toward keeping a healthy relationship. The couple talked about how…

- Sometimes we need to be told when we're wrong.

- Sometimes we need to be told we look good.

- Sometimes we need to know when we did the right thing.

*

A brief breakfast turned into a deep conversation, but a fun one. You've realized power couples can give great advice, like the importance of earning respect and communicating clearly.

Who is one **power couple** you'd like to learn from?

_____

_____

***

Why Are You Worth It?

For this story, put yourself in a similar situation where you approach someone you like, want to learn from, or just simply want to talk to. Some examples could be in settings such as a bar, the store, work, or any social scene.

*

It's been a fantastic day, and you find yourself at the bar celebrating life and looking to meet new people. Maybe a future significant other!

After you find someone you're interested in talking to, a welcoming "hello" and introduction come shortly afterward. A couple of sentences are exchanged before you get asked why are you worth it (as in talking to)?

This statement came out of nowhere, and after thinking for a second, your comeback is, "I care, I am a good person, I am loyal, I am cool, and I am fun to be around."

After that, the conversation goes okay, but there's not much connection.

*

Later that night, you realize when asked,

"Why are you worth talking to?"

You didn't once mention the other person! You simply said, "I am" over and over. Of course, there was no connection after that because there was no value given back.

What if you sparked interest with this person by saying something like…

I'll help you be a better version of yourself, how great do you want to be?

You now sound confident and like you have their best interest in mind, which gives this person a reason to want to talk to you and enlightens a conversation that can now dive deeper.

You have now earned respect, and this person can see the value in talking to you and getting to know you further.

***

Age Is Just a Number

Why is it that you sometimes get along with a person much older or younger than you?

Many will admit their best friend is their daughter, son, mother, or father.

The truth is, sometimes, being friends with people of a variety of ages is a great way to see different perspectives, enjoy different activities, and have experiences that won't usually happen with your typical friends.

Respect can be earned at all ages; how you choose to look at that is up to you. Before judging someone by their age, maybe try looking at them through their experiences, their personality traits, and their interests.

Remember, the more true friends you have, the more opportunities you'll have.

*

What will you do to make sure you give people a chance to become your friend?

_____
_____
_____

Loyalty

Authentic Nature, Genuine Compliments, and Honest Feedback

It's lunchtime, your stomach's ready for fuel, and your mind's ready for a break. But earlier today, you committed to meet your friend for lunch an hour from now! Even though you're starving and want to eat immediately, you decide to wait it out and follow through on your promise.

*

An hour passes, and finally, it's time to meet your friend at the Café. Brief hellos are exchanged, and you give a genuine compliment, "Hey Liz, I like your watch, where did you get it?"

The conversation has an immediate spark, and your friend explains anything and everything about the watch.

With this compliment, you have shown interest in your friend and have given an open-ended question to help ensure a fluid conversation going forward.

*

As you're eating this lifesaving lunch, it becomes apparent your friend has a piece of ketchup that didn't make it to their mouth.

Do you say something or let it go?

Put yourself in their shoes, would you want someone to tell you if you had ketchup on your chin?

Of course, you would! As embarrassing as it is, this happens.

True friends speak up when needed, true friends are authentic, and true friends show their loyalty through words and actions.

They **follow through on promises**.

They give **genuine compliments**.

They are **authentic** and **speak up when needed**.

***

Following Through on Promises

For this story, think about these thoughts separately and briefly.

*

You committed to going on a date that you don't want to go on.

*

You told a friend you'd give her your Justin Bieber tickets at face value, but you see they are going for double that price for resale online.

*

You got offered a dream day trip in NYC but have a board meeting at work that day…

*

What would you do in these situations?

The truth is, it's ultimately up to you.

Do you want to be known as the person who can't be counted on, always bails, and is unreliable?

Or

Do you want to build trust and follow through on your promises?

Following through on your **promises** may not always be the favored choice, the easiest to get through, or the most exciting. But following through on promises **builds trust**. You never know when you'll need that person you had a prior commitment to.

***

Another Wedding, Can You Say No?

It's a Tuesday evening, and you're catching up with a friend for dinner. You don't see this friend very often, and the conversation starts like any other. After catching up and enjoying a couple glasses of wine, your friend goes into a rant about her "bridesmaid burn out."

She's been in seven weddings this year and has three more on the horizon. As you know, weddings don't come cheap (and not just for the bride and groom). As she laments about the significant commitment of time and money required by these weddings, you begin to wonder: If it's so taxing for her, why does she commit?

Is it for her desire to be respected? Is it for her desire for reciprocity at her wedding? Is it to be a good friend? Is it to feed her ego?

Or is it her inability to say **no**?

*

When is the right time to say **no**, how do you say **no**, and what will happen if you say **no**?

This concept is something continuously faced in social settings, whether it's with a date, with alcohol and drugs, at work, or something you do not want to make time for.

*

What will happen if you say **no**?

Have you ever played out the other side of the situation?

Is it possible that the bride had too many bridesmaids anyways and felt obligated to include you?

*

Saying **no** might not always be a good or bad thing. But how will you know if you don't take time to think about the other side of things?

Is it worth spending $10,000 this year for other people's weddings?

Could that money be spent differently and lead to something bigger and better for your future?

Making a list of core values you want to live by may make decisions like these more manageable.

What is one core value that you will represent? If you don't understand the meaning of a core value, list a trait that you would like people to think of when thinking of you.

_____

Being Present

Relationships Are More Important Than Schedules

Your friend recently broke up with her long-time boyfriend. She calls you during this heartbreak and doesn't know what to do. She's crying, pissed off, and ready to kill her ex. Little does she know you have a major presentation at work tomorrow, and you don't have much time. But you understand relationships are more important than schedules and make time to listen.

By listening and giving her guidance throughout the conversation, you bring value to the friendship and get a thank you for consoling her.

Since she lives far away, but to keep things positive and to take initiative, you promise to send her a care package. In the box is a picture of the both of you at a Taylor Swift concert five years ago, a couple of her favorite candy bars, and a handwritten note saying you will visit her in a month.

*

After getting the care package, she calls you and expresses how grateful she is to have you as a friend.

*

Since the breakup, things have calmed down, and it's time for you to visit. That weekend you'll have the time of your life popping bottles, dancing till your shoes fall off, and enjoying the quality time together.

Your ability to listen, take initiative, make time, express positivity, show a caring nature, stay loyal, follow through on promises, and communicate clearly allowed her to transition away from her ex. She has seen the value you brought to the friendship and said that if there is ever anything you need, she's got your back!

Relationships are more important than schedules. **Make time** and **be present**!

***

Dress to Impress

After being a couple of years into the working field, you are still trying to earn respect for a pay raise, job promotion, more units, more productivity, and more clients. You start to wonder why what you're doing isn't working. One trend you've noticed over the years is your boss is always the best-dressed person in the room.

A few days later, the opportunity to speak one-on-one with your boss comes up, in the conversation you mention that you've noticed how sharp, clean-cut, and professional he dresses.

Your boss says…

"Thank you. I committed to present myself in a way where people take me seriously, where they know they're in good hands, and that I'm the best person to go to. Along with being present through active listening, the appearance you give someone is the other half of the sale. If you want to be taken seriously, get your clothes fitted, stay clean-cut, and look as professional as possible. You will make more money and have more opportunities arise. If you want to be great, commit to making the way you present yourself a priority."

What does "professionally dressed" mean to you?

_____

_____

What's one way you can improve your appearance?

_____

_____

***

Be Present, Meet Someone New

 You're in the far corner of a room filled with two hundred industry professionals waiting for the speaker to start his talk. Thinking this will be another time-wasting event, you start scrolling through Instagram until the speaker, who is known for his emotional rants, yells out,

"Get off your phone and meet someone new."

After looking up for the first time since walking into the room, it's obvious you weren't the only one being anti-social. Deciding it might be in your best interest to listen to the speaker, you slowly get up to find someone to talk with, and eye contact is made with the lady behind you. You're welcomed with a smile as hands reach out, and names are exchanged, you both hit it off despite the significant age difference.

*

Is it that easy to start a conversation? The answer is more complicated then it may seem, because going out of a comfort zone puts you in a state of discomfort, question, and worry. What happens in the conversation could make or break your day. If there's an awkward silence, you may be embarrassed, and then if there is a smile or compliment your day could be made!

No one has ever made a shot they didn't take. Who knows what connections can be developed from a conversation with a stranger, what opportunities could arise, or what feelings could be exchanged. They may be good chats, or they may not be. But why not meet new people and try?

Remember, people equal opportunities. Take advantage when they are around, be present, and don't be afraid to go out of your comfort zone.

***

Learning How to Communicate Is Essential in Life

What is one class high school and colleges offer that applies to the real world?

In my opinion, this would be speech class. You may or may not agree.

Every day, humans communicate with family and friends, significant others, and co-workers. Learning how to communicate appropriately with those people is essential to living a life on your terms. If you want to be told what to do for the rest of your life, then you may not need to work on this skill. But if you've made it this far in the book, chances are you are ready to make big things happen.

*

In school, we're often told what to do, when to do it, and how to do it, which leads to the issue of an obvious lack of interest from many students. This is not always the case, but it often is.

When people find topics they are interested in, they spend hours upon hours trying to figure out, learn, and master that subject.

*

What if it was a requirement for schools to have speech classes focused on learning how to speak publicly based on the student's interest? In this class, instead of taking a test that students study hours for, only to forget the information days later, why not learn from people in their field of interest? After learning from people in their field, the final exam would consist of each student giving a presentation on what they learned.

How valuable would that class be – a class solely focused on real-world application through learning from people of interest and explaining what was learned?

***

If Tomorrow Never Came

If tomorrow never came, how great would today have been?

It may be a tough question or make you realize that this moment right now may be the best time to be alive, to enjoy, to cherish, and to be present.

Why is this? It's because who knows what tomorrow will bring. Right here, right now is a great time to be alive, to go after what you want, and to enjoy what you can.

A lack of motivation is one thing, but when the time comes

that you'll no longer be alive. Don't you want to say you gave it your all, did what you wanted, and you lived it up?

Or would you rather say, I wish I did _____ and/or only if I _____?

*

Being present daily can lead to a life of meaning, impact, and fulfillment with far fewer regrets.

What's one thing you can do to be more present today?

_____

_____

***

Focusing on the Now to Create a Better Future You

It's understandable to worry, get distracted, and procrastinate. Things happen to shift us away from our goals, and this happens when you move away from the present.

With your health, there was that one time Jimmy told you, just one more drink, and who could forget dinner last weekend when Debbie told you to live a little and have dessert.

People have influence, sometimes for the good and sometimes not for any good. By staying focused on the present and surrounding yourself with people who positively influence your life, it will be easier to do what is needed to get your desired result.

One way to positively influence your health and stay present is to find a workout partner. It will help with accountability, consistency, and commitment. It's tougher to skip a day when someone else is counting on you.

*

Regarding relationships, the build-up to your first date with Casey next weekend has got you nervous, anxious, and worried.

These are normal thoughts on the build-up to the first date, and one way to take the pressure off of you is to prepare. Preparation helps to stay focused on what needs to be done instead of worrying about the outcome.

Instead of worrying for three full days leading up to the date, whether Casey will like you or not, maybe it would be better to read/learn about good questions to ask on a date, how to become a better listener, or how to nail the first impression.

*

Preparation helps focus on what needs to be done for the desired outcome and directly applies to the development of wealth.

Many people want to make a lot of money, have financial freedom, and move up in their companies.

But things happen. The day before your team presentation in front of your boss, Judith informs you and your team she didn't do her part of the deal. She is resigning from the company and wishes you the best. You can now choose to worry about what your boss is going to say, drop the pitch, and blame it on Judith, or you can focus on what can be done to help finish it.

*

Being present helps relieve stress from worrying about failure and helps focus on what needs to be done to make great things happen.

Taking Ownership

The Painfully Awesome Mistake

In 2015, Steve Harvey was announcing the winner of the Miss Universe Pageant, and he said the wrong name!

Whether it was his fault or not is irrelevant. When he found out the wrong name was called, he knew a mistake had been made, and it needed to be fixed.

For a variety of reasons, he was told not to go back out on stage. But he decided to do the right thing and announce to the audience a mistake was made. He got heckled for the error but took ownership and made things right.

*

Forty-eight hours later, his name had been googled four billion times.

With attention come opportunities. The more people who know about you, the more money you'll be able to make. If you don't believe me, go back to the "Building Your Network" story in the Creating Opportunities section of the book.

Since attention is directly correlated to net worth, this mistake he owned up to, may have been the most beneficial one of his career.

Owning up to your mistakes may not always work out with results like this, but owning up to your mistakes gives you an opportunity to make things right. And when you make things right, you **earn respect**.

***

Taking Initiative Helps Create Opportunities

While putting your groceries into your car, you see some misplaced carts.

What do you do?

Do you pack up your groceries and let the carts stay where they are because you didn't put them there?

Or

Do you accept responsibility and put the shopping carts away?

There isn't a right answer here, but accepting responsibility and putting them away is the same concept that will help you earn respect with everyday activities.

If you drop a crumb on the ground, own up to it and pick it up instead of leaving it on the ground for someone else to pick up. You never know who's watching.

When you're late for work, own up to it and say, "Thank you for your patience" to your clients, co-workers, or bosses instead of making an excuse. If you're already late, don't waste people's time by making excuses.

If you forget to do your homework for school or work, own up to it and find out what can be done now to make up for your mistake.

When you take ownership, you give yourself an opportunity to solve problems instead of creating them.

EXCEL

Take Time to Think

Jeff Bezos (founder of Amazon) has a creative approach to start his day. It may come to a surprise he takes his time to get up and running for the day…to think, get settled in, and get ready for what's coming ahead.

Thinking leads to planning and preparing for what you want, which leads to a **feeling** that you can and will do something. Which is then followed by an **action**, and with appropriate action, you can have **massive results**. This process together helps with **accelerating forward** from point A to B.

*

Taking time to think can be done in a variety of ways, such as meditating, going for a walk, lying in bed, or going to a quiet place where no one is around.

Where would be a good spot for you to take time to think?

_____

_____

Now take some time to think…

How did it feel?

_____

_____

What did you think about?

_____

_____

What are some thoughts you felt like acting on?

_____

_____

What's one action step you can take toward those thoughts?

_____

_____

***

Separating Yourself with a Solid Resumé

It's time for a fresh start, a new job, a new place, and new co-workers. After spending weeks searching, applying, and receiving only a few responses, it becomes evident that your resumé needs to get cleaned up.

You update your resumé and have a friend look it over. Within seconds, your friend says, "Your resumé is boring!"

You think, "Boring, I made it look picture-perfect." Your friend explains, "The credentials may be good, but it won't stick out. Make it more appealing by using computer technology and thinking in the mindset of an employer. It's easy for the employer to remember you when your resumé has a professional headshot and is easy to read. It gives you a better chance of being remembered, shows your ability to prepare and think outside of the box, and interest in the job."

*

Great businesses are always looking for great people.

Stepping it up with a great resumé is one way to stick out and accelerate your career.

***

Why Truly Busy People Always Get the Job Done

Work has been going all right, but financially you're not where you want to be. Frustrated is an understatement because you aren't getting the big-ticket task(s). What's more disappointing is your co-employee Bob keeps getting all the work.

Wondering why this is happening, you ask your boss why Bob keeps getting all the critical tasks.

Your boss explains that he understands where you are coming from and would like to help solve your discomfort and frustration.

He explains, "When there is something important that needs to be done, I go to the busiest person because I know they will get the job done and are a trusted source.

"Bob does certain things well, like finding things to do instead of waiting, he asks good questions that make us think about things we could do better, and makes our jobs easier by checking in to see if we need anything."

You thank your boss for his time and begin to put a lot of thought into what he said and decide to figure out ways to take initiative going forward.

First, you start to look for ways to help Bob and for ways to spend more time around him. Spending time around him will allow you to see what he does well and help take tasks off his shoulders.

Second, you decide to make it a point every day to say hello to your boss and give one positive comment with every encounter, whether it's a funny joke, something you like about the company, or giving your boss a hint about a future task that you want.

Bob creates opportunities, and so can you.

Relating this to your work, what are three things you can do to be more productive?

1.) _____
_____

2.) _____
_____

3.) _____
_____

**

What We Wish We Knew Then

Being out in the real world for the first time strikes you hard, like a slap in the face from a drunk at the bar…unexpected, harsh, and annoying.

Being stubborn in the past, when your parents and teachers tried to teach you, has fully backfired!

You're officially a grown-up, and new things are getting

discovered daily. For example, you start to realize some things, such as,

Starting the washer for the first time isn't as easy as you thought.

Food doesn't get cooked just sitting there.

Flat tires don't blow up as easy as a balloon.

Saying hi to the person next to you can lead to a job you've always wanted.

Properly brushing your teeth can save you $300 on a cavity.

That saying please and thank you can lead to making someone's day.

*

It's important to explore different things before picking the right job, the right person, or the right active lifestyle.

There are many things we wish we knew growing up, but unfortunately, some of us were not taught or were too stubborn to listen to our parents/guardians/teachers about the real world.

*

You have an opportunity to learn from your mistakes and from other people's mistakes to excel forward and learn.

What are you grateful for being taught growing up?

_____

_____

What do you wish you were taught growing up? Why?

_____
_____

Moving forward, how can you learn from what you wish you were taught and become more self-aware about listening to the right people?

_____
_____
_____

Growth

Create Your Own University

Often students have dreams. Joe, in particular, wanted to become the best golf coach in the world. He knew there was a lot to learn, and school wasn't cutting it, so he made a list of the top ten golf coaches he could learn from.

After making his list, he concluded the best way to learn from each coach was to meet each one in person and to observe him or her teaching.

To take action, he started searching for contact information, sent dozens of emails, and worked toward making the contacts necessary to meet each coach.

*

The first trip was set, and Joe found a golf coach about ninety minutes from school. A couple of days before going to observe, the coach informed him there are a few conditions:

1.) Please dress professionally, iron your clothes, wear dark-colored pants and shoes, and a collared shirt without distracting patterns like stripes and dots.
2.) You will be introduced to the person taking the lesson. After that, please do not talk unless asked a question. I can answer any questions you have after the lesson is finished.
3.) Do not cross your arms or put hands in your pockets. When someone sees this, that person will typically think you're bored, don't want to be talked to, or don't want to be there.

4.)   When the lesson is complete, make sure you thank the person who let you observe.

*

The lesson went well, making the trip a success. Over the next five years, Joe observed each coach on his list and essentially created his own university. Throughout the five years, Joe started implementing what he learned to anyone who would listen. After two years, he started getting people to pay him for golf lessons, and three years later, he was running his own teaching business.

*

Creating your own university and learning from the best will allow rapid growth to happen. I call this the Point A to Point B approach.

What is the fastest way to get from Point A to Point B?

A straight line, right?

Yep! Even though there may be bumps, roadblocks, and flat tires along the way. With this approach, you will have accelerated the learning process and set yourself up for a bright future in the industry you want to succeed in!

Who are the top ten people you'd like to learn from?

1.)
2.)
3.)
4.)
5.)
6.)
7.)

8.)
9.)
10.)

***

Breakfast with Your Mentor, What do You Want?

Success is starting to come your way, and you're making enough money to live a good life and starting to figure things out. But you're still not where you want to be, which has led you to continue to learn, observe, and take action to better yourself.

Eager to learn, you focus on setting up breakfast with someone you want to meet. You decide on trying to set up breakfast because it's quick, everyone has to eat, and there isn't much to lose by trying. After sending five emails and calling your mentor's office ten times, you finally get in contact with her assistant, who suggests that you go to her conference in four weeks, and if you do, you can have breakfast with her.

*

Four weeks go by; anticipation and excitement build as you arrive at breakfast. Your clothes are ironed, matching, and you look like you could be on the front cover of a magazine.

As you sit down, the waiter puts down a couple of menus. Your mentor gives hers right back, and orders two eggs scrambled, two pieces of bacon, and one piece of rye toast.

There is no name for this on the menu, but you don't think much of it and order one of the daily specials. After wondering why your mentor ordered nothing on the menu, an interesting conversation arises…

You: Do you always order food like that? As in entrees that aren't listed on the menu?

Mentor: Yes, why did you order what you did?

You: Well, it looked good, and I am starving.

Mentor: I agree, that does look and sound good. But how are you ever going to get what you want if you don't know what you want?

You: …speechless…thinking…

Mentor: I ordered what I did because I know what I want. Knowing what foods make me feel well and energized saves time, keeps my energy levels where they need to be, and puts me in a position to succeed for the rest of the day.

Knowing what you want helps you prepare for what needs to be done to get what you want.

*

You're blown away and realize the importance of knowing what you want.

After breakfast settles in and taking time to think, it becomes evident that to get what you want; it's essential to know what you want and to prepare for it.

What do you want? (No need to answer this question right now, just something to think about)

***

Feeling Trapped, What Do I Do?

Your job isn't cutting it for you. The pay is okay, but growth with the company has stayed stagnant for the last two years, and you feel little excitement going to work. Even though you hate your job, you feel like it's necessary to stay because of your student loans, rent, and that trip to Australia.

Feeling trapped and bored, and finding yourself continually saying, "I can't wait to quit," what do you do?

Do you ask your boss at work for advice? Do you ask family members for advice? Do you suck it up and not say anything?

Or

Do you ask someone you look up to for advice that has had success, who has been in a similar situation and can positively influence your decision?

*

When thinking about who to reach out to, your former boss Alex comes to mind. The next day you call him, and he says, "It's normal to be doing something you don't like when you're young and haven't built up wealth.

"Just because you're working a job you don't like, that doesn't mean you can't spend your off hours working on one you do like. Write down five people you admire, respect, or maybe even potentially want to be like.

"Once those five names are written down, learn from them through reading their books, taking them out to lunch, paying for their time, or by anything else you can think of.

"To **get** what you're looking for, you have to **ask,** and once you start **asking**, you start discovering **answers** and **creating opportunities**.

"Remember that life is precious, and that time is the most important asset we all have. Be sure to use it wisely."

*

Who are five people you'd like to learn from?

Health Related…

1.)_____
2.)_____
3.)_____
4.)_____
5.)_____

Wealth Related…

1.)_____
2.)_____
3.)_____
4.)_____
5.)_____

Relationships Related…

1.)_____
2.)_____
3.)_____
4.)_____
5.)_____

***

The 10X Rule

Grant Cardone is well-known for writing a book called *The 10X Rule*. It's a book based on the concept of multiplying massively to help 10X your **business**, 10X your **income**, and 10X your **life**.

Think about this for a minute…

What is a way you can make $10?

Okay, great, now do that ten more times, and you get $100.

Now do that ten more times, and you get $1,000.

Do that ten more times, and you get $10,000.

Even better, do that ten more times, and you get $100,000.

Awesome, now do that ten more times, and you get $1,000,000.

Accumulating a million dollars may not be simple as listed above, but the 10X mindset will help you think of what needs to be done to get where you want.

*

What are ten things you enjoy doing?

Great! Do those ten times more and watch the things you hate start to fade away.

*

What are ten things your significant other likes?

Great! Do those ten times more and see what happens to your relationship.

Who are ten people you enjoy spending time with?

Great! Spend more time around those people and see what happens to your friendships.

*

What are ten ways you like to stay active?

What are ten healthy dishes you enjoy eating?

Great, do those things and eat those dishes more often and see what happens to your health.

*

The 10X Rule is a mindset, and it's not about the actual number itself. It's about **thinking big** and **achieving big**.

***

Nothing in Nature Blossoms Year Round

It's springtime, and the rain is pouring.

Day…

After day…

After day.

When is it ever going to stop?!

As Cinco de Mayo comes around, the flowers start

blossoming, and the sun is even staying out past 7:30 PM!

*

If April showers bring May flowers, then what happens the other ten months of the year?

Things in nature don't blossom year-round, and many die in the winter. For example, cold weather causes things like flowers to stop growing. But when they get what's needed, they blossom nicely. Flowers absorb nutrients to grow, then blossom and shine, before freezing and deflating for the winter, only to start all over when winter ends.

Even bears hibernate in the winter to conserve energy, rest, and re-fuel. Then, when the weather gets nicer, they roam around and do what bears do.

*

There's a famous quote, "If you're not growing, you're dying." Although this may make sense, it's impossible to keep growing without encountering bumps in the road. Flowers have nature to work around. Humans have factors to work through as well, like work, family, and unexpected life events.

There may be days, weeks, and seasons of minimal to no growth, and hearing things like **no**, **you failed**, and **you didn't make it** may be tough to hear. But sometimes these roadblocks help encourage growth and push you in the right direction going forward.

***

Learning to Sell to Get What You Want

To be in the relationship of your dreams, it's essential to sell yourself to your "future" husband or wife with why he or she should be with you.

For example, to go on a date with someone, that person must see value in you to agree. For someone to be in a relationship with you, this person would need a reason to commit to being your boyfriend or girlfriend. When marriage looks like an option, the other person would need to be sold that you're the best person in the world for him or her.

*

In business, sales are often thought of as bad or annoying. But if your sales will help other people, then it's almost a disservice if you don't sell your product or service. It important to sell products and services, but it's also necessary to sell yourself to future employees, business partners, or anyone else that may help you increase revenue. Because increased revenue equals increased sales, and with increased sales, you're able to help more people.

*

To achieve true happiness, it's important to sell yourself through personal fulfillment, accomplishment, and achievements.

Fulfillment comes through taking action on things you want to accomplish or achieve, for example, checking off an item on your bucket list.

*

What's one thing you can do to work on your sales skills?

_____

_____

_____

**

What Ever Happened to the Kid Who Just Went for It?

Think back to when you were younger and wanted to learn how to ride a bike. The training wheels got plopped on, and the pedaling started. Before you knew it, the extra wheels were useless. After trying a hundred plus times, you made it across the entire driveway!

*

How about when you wanted to build a treehouse and started gathering wood, then bought a hammer and nails, and started building.

*

Remember the tree you wanted to climb but didn't know how? And, without much thought, you grabbed the sides and reached for the branch above and kept climbing till you made it toward the top.

*

When you go for things, you start paving a path for yourself to figure things out. By taking action, taking initiative, and pursuing challenges, you start building a life on your terms.

What is one challenge that you can start taking action on today?

_____

_____

_____

Greatness

Meeting the Person You Want to Be

A conference can be thought of as being mandatory, an opportunity to learn, or an atmosphere to connect with like-minded people.

Regardless of the reason behind going to a conference, if you're there, why not make the most out if it?

*

For this story, put yourself in the shoes of the person at the conference…

Las Vegas, the city of sins, and lost wages! It's hard to believe you traveled across the country to go to a conference in the party city of the world. At the conference, it's safe to say there will be plenty of light bulb ideas because there are twenty speakers set to speak.

*

The conference goes well, but you're overwhelmed by the information shared over the three days. After taking time to let the information settle, there's one concept you can't get off your mind. On the second day, a speaker got up on stage whom you've never heard of. He looked about forty-five years old, in excellent shape, and a model of confidence. He brought the energy, fired the crowd up, and began his speech by telling a story.

He talked about how at the end of his life, he'd like to meet the identical twin that he never had but knew everything about. He hoped to know everything about this twin because it would mean he lived up to his potential and became the person he was supposed to be.

After some thought, you realize on top of making money, being a caring family member, and staying healthy, that it's also important to live up to your potential and make a positive impact.

*

If your life ended right now, how would you be remembered? What would people think of you?

These may be tough questions to think about…

Are you satisfied with your answers?

If not, what will you do to work on satisfying those answers?

_____

_____

***

The Guy Everyone Loved

To touch on the story above, there was a guy who loved his community, religion, and family. He was always trying to get people together, play music, and pass on his lifelong message of living a life filled with joy and happiness.

He knew his life was going to be judged by how the people around him were doing. If they were having fun, he was. If the people around him were boring and negative, he knew he'd trend toward that direction. His mission in life was to help the people around him do well, have fun, and enjoy life.

He married a kind-hearted woman who was a waitress at the local restaurant, one of those waitresses you always look forward to seeing and the whole town knows. Together they raised an amazing son, who seemed to have an endless number of friends at school, not necessarily from popularity but because he was a good guy. He was one of those kids that, every time you saw him, you felt positive vibes and a genuine conversation ahead. Together they were a strong, fun, and joyful family. But the father wanted more.

He was on the board off various non-profit organizations, always coached and helped out his son's sports teams, and hosted numerous community events, where he played live music and got many of the patrons from the community together.

He was considered a local legend for bringing life to the community. He was the guy everyone could turn to for advice and the guy who would play fantastic music performances with his beloved band.

After he got sick and passed away after sixty years of age, his life was weirdly just starting because he made an impact.

After his passing, messages kept flowing from friends, family, co-workers, and people he brought value to throughout his lifetime.

The reason his life had just started, was that instead of sadness and sorrow, he brought joy and good memories back to everyone who thought of him after passing away. His impact was widespread throughout the community, and an unannounced person he impacted through his values decided to build a statue for him, near the park where he had performed often.

Every time someone walks by the statue, they are reminded

of what making a difference in the community means and the positive traits of a role model.

***

150 People Funeral Test

This story tags along with the previous two. Answer the following questions with an open mind.

When life's over…

How will you be remembered?

_____
_____
_____

What will people say about you?

_____
_____
_____

Who will show up at your funeral?

_____
_____
_____

These questions may be hard to think about, but it will help you realize the impact you want to have and who the real friends are in your life.

Would you rather have people celebrate your life for the joy you brought to them or have them be at your funeral because they had to?

An excellent way to think about this could be: will there be at least 150 people at my funeral?

This is a concept I learned from Tai Lopez, and it's to get you thinking about impact. The number of 150 doesn't matter as much as the idea behind the thought. You can still live a great life without 150 showing up to your funeral, but imagine the amount of value you would have brought if 150 or more people showed up to celebrate your life. Muhammad Ali, Nelson Mandela, Martin Luther King Jr., Mother Teresa, and Gandhi are great examples of leaders who had thousands show up to celebrate their life, accomplishments, and impact.

***

When You Do More Than You're Paid, Eventually You'll Be Paid More Than You Do

It's a beautiful day, and you decide to go for a walk in the park, where you see a long line near a lady painting pictures. After asking around to see what the heck is going on, you find out it's a famous artist painting pictures. Naturally, you decide to wait in line to get yours.

You're finally up, and the artist starts painting your picture. The setting is calm, quiet, and your eyes are glued to every brush she takes. The masterpiece is finished, and she hands you the painting. She says, "Here you go, that will be $3,000."

You: "$3,000, that took you three minutes!"

Painter: "No, that took me thirty years to make it in three minutes."

*

Mastery may take time, but it can be developed through hard work, dedication, and passion. Mastering skills that bring value to people may take years, but when developed, you'll be able to charge a heck of a lot more. Only the greats, like the painter above, can charge and sell for that much in such a short amount of time.

What's often not talked about is the hundreds of thousands of paintings done before that. Many before that were done for no return with hours, weeks, months, and years of effort. But, with that effort, the ability to create a masterpiece like the one above was developed.

No one in the world could have painted the picture as this lady did. Her paintings were unique, and she had one concept that pushed her through the tough times, which was: "When you do more than you're paid, eventually you'll be paid more than you do."

***

Prepare Properly or Prepare to Fail

It's April of 2019, and the Masters golf tournament is happening!

Tiger Woods has a chance of making the greatest comeback ever.

He's in the final group, in contention, and wearing his Sunday red. As he walks to the first tee, it looks like you could throw a rock at him, and he wouldn't flinch.

Celebrities are on the course everywhere, from NFL quarterbacks to Olympic champions, to billionaires. What a scene it is.

As you're following Tiger on the course, you notice to the left of you is an NFL starting quarterback observing, hanging out, and staying low key with no one bothering him.

You start wondering if you should ask him a question, say hi, give a compliment, dab up, or not say anything and walk away.

*

Put yourself in a similar situation and think of someone famous you'd like to ask a question to...

If you saw that person randomly, what would be the question you'd ask? How could you word the question, so that this person sees the value in answering back?

_____

_____

_____

*

Back on the course, after brainstorming for five minutes about what to say, you finally come up with a question, a question that you'd get value out of, and may bring value back to the other person.

You ask: "What is the difference between preparing for an NFL game on Sunday and preparing for the final round of the Masters?"

He says: "I feel like the biggest difference is you can prepare more for the final round of the Masters because in football there are ten other teammates on the field with you, plus another eleven playing against you, with many random things happening throughout the game."

The conversation ends there, and it was a successful one because you went for it and had a conversation.

*

Later that day, you find out Tiger Woods said he was waking up at 3:45 AM for a 9:20 AM tee time. That's a lot of preparation time before playing a five-hour round of golf!

Throughout the round, Tiger continues to look fearless, and the field starts to fade. Eventually leading to a historic day as Tiger wins his 15th major and 5th green jacket.

*

Is Tiger the best because he prepares, practices, and works harder than anyone else? Or is it natural talent and luck that makes him so great.

Do Bill Belichick, Tom Brady, and the rest of the Patriots prepare, practice, and play better than everyone? Or is it luck and talent that led them to six Super Bowl victories in eighteen years?

*

There is a common trend between preparation and success, whether it's in golf, team sports, relationships, entertainment, or business.

"By failing to prepare, you are preparing to fail."
– Ben Franklin

***

Having Fun

What Risks Should Be Taken in Life?

What better way to spend your last summer before graduating college than living and working in NYC? What a time to be alive and what a place to be.

*

After you settle into NYC, the coffee shop across the street becomes your go-to spot. One day, as you are slowly savoring your Frappuccino, one of the employees at the shop asks if you are going to see Stevie Wonder play at Central Park tonight.

Not having known about this leaves you in a state of shock! It has been on your bucket list for years to see Stevie Wonder, and you're determined to go tonight, even though tickets are sold out.

After convincing a friend to go with you in the hope of buying tickets from scalpers at the entrance, you have no luck. Still determined to find a way in, the only option left is to walk around Central Park and see if there is a way to sneak in. Throughout the heart-racing walk, you find a fence to climb over.

Do you risk getting in trouble or kicked out, not to mention numerous cuts and bruises? Or do you go home without a fight, knowing you may never have the chance to see Stevie Wonder again?

Of course, you go for it, and you think what's life if you don't go out of your comfort zone and chase after experiences.

Without hesitating, you and your friend climb over the fence and walk a mile to the concert where Stevie Wonder is minutes away from coming on stage. As he plays throughout the night, positive vibes are present everywhere through dancing and sing-along songs.

*

You took a risk, marked an experience off your bucket list, and had the time of your life. Was it unethical to sneak into the concert? It probably was, but you had a fantastic time, no one got hurt, and you checked off an item on your bucket list.

*

The point of this story is not to contrast other values in the book or to be unethical; it's to emphasize that successful people take risks. I'm not saying to jump over fences and do things that shouldn't be done. What's important to understand is the concept of finding a way to get what you want, and figuring out how to get through the roadblocks to get there.

***

Speak Up When Something Is Wrong

An essential part of having fun, keeping stress low, and genuinely being happy is to **speak up** when something is wrong.

*

If you have three roommates and one of them never does the dishes, what do you do?

Do you speak up or let it go and hold in the frustration?

*

If you're under the weather and can't seem to figure out what's wrong, do you speak up and talk to a doctor or sit there wondering what's wrong?

*

If you're jobless, broke, and have no money in your bank account, do you sit there and wish you had money, or do you speak up and ask for a job?

*

Understandably, it may feel hard and out of your comfort zone to speak up, but it's crucial to when something is wrong because if you speak up when things aren't right, you'll likely be a lot happier.

What's something you need to **speak up** about?

_____
_____
_____

***

Do You Celebrate, Do You Validate?

Working hard to accomplish something great brings different feelings and emotions. From the feeling of winning a championship that you never want to end, to wondering why people celebrate the day you were born.

One way to look at celebrating would be, "Why not?"

Celebration gives opportunities for people to come together positively. Whether a celebration happens because of hard work, teamwork, family, or friends, it gives you time to enjoy the "ups" of life. A chance to embrace the tough times and enjoy the present.

Validation helps affirm your accomplishments and shows how people feel about you. Has saying congrats ever gotten someone mad? Probably not too many.

Celebration and validation give us a feeling of accomplishment, excitement, and achievement. Of course, you should celebrate your accomplishments, whether it's for thirty seconds or thirty years is up to you.

***

Work Should Be Fun

It's been a long day, the ticks on the clock feel like they're going slower than ever! Every day you dread going into work and look forward to leaving more than anything.

Why is this?

Is it because you hate work? Your boss doesn't give you enough responsibility? You get stressed out every time your co-worker messes up?

Or

Is it because work is just not fun?

*

A common question asked in the social scene is, "What do you do for work?" Like most people, you probably get sick and tired of answering that question because it's a long answer, the person asking probably won't understand what you do or doesn't care and won't listen.

Instead of asking what someone does, wouldn't it be appropriate to first ask if he/or she enjoys what he/or she does for work?

After all, work takes up a significant part of someone's day.

*

What about you? Do you enjoy what you do for work?

If so, why?

If not, why not?

*

There's will always be things that aren't interesting at work. Along with tasks at home (chores), like taking out the trash and doing dishes. But if you can find work that feels like a lifestyle and fun, you'd probably agree there would be a lot of fulfillment in your life.

What type of work is fun to you that feels like a lifestyle?

_____

_____

_____

***

What Was Life Like Before Cell Phones?

Did people…

Say hi and smile at each other when walking by instead of looking down at their phone and scrolling through social media?

Dance with each other at clubs instead of dancing to their phones with kissy faces and showcasing their colorful drinks?

Wait for you when you were running five minutes late instead of feeling like a "running five minutes late" text has to be sent?

*

What would life be like if you put your phone away? What do you have to lose if you try it? You'll be amazed at the people you meet, the conversations you take part in, and the unforgettable experiences you have!

This is a concept I touched on twice in this book for a reason. Hint-Hint, try going without a cell phone for a night out, a day, or even an hour!

How did it feel?

_____

_____

What was it like?

_____

_____

Why would you or wouldn't you try this again?

_____

_____

***

The 12 "C" Words Toward Excelling Forward

You're up early getting a workout in, and feeling good this morning when you notice a familiar face in the gym. Someone of meaning, someone who's done well in life, and someone that may be able to give you valuable advice.

Since you're feeling good today, you decide to approach this person by saying your name and asking if he is a business owner.

It turns out you're talking to the youngest person ever to own a fortune 500 company!

Wow...

Knowing his time is valuable, and you may only have thirty seconds of his time, the one question you ask is:

"Knowing what you know now, what advice would you give to young professionals trying to make it in business and life?"

He explains how it's important to treat the four pillars of life equally, which are **health, wealth, relationships,** and **happiness**.

You thank him for his advice and get on with the rest of your workout.

*

What he said sounded simple, but left you thinking about how important it is to pursue more aspects of life than just work, just love, just health, or just happiness.

*

After deciding to take time and think about these individually, you end up coming up with values to help fulfill them equally:

Wealth

CONNECT: With clients, customers, and employees. Be present when talking to people. Actively listen to keep conversations fun and productive.

COMMIT: The 10-year rule is famous for explaining how it takes ten years or 10,000 hours to master a skill. Without commitment, you won't be able to get through the tough times, but with a commitment, you will be able to achieve great things in life.

CARE: It's important to care about yourself, so you can care enough to help others.

Health

CONSISTENT: With consistency and a proper diet/workout/mindset plan, you'll have a significantly increased chance of getting the body you want, being more productive, and of getting the outcome you want. Without consistency, it will be tough to stay focused and committed to what you are trying to accomplish.

CLEAR: It's important to be clear with goals, with your plan, and with the direction you want to go in moving forward.

CONFIDENCE: Taking care of your body and promoting a positive active lifestyle through words and actions will help build physical and mental health.

Relationships

COMPLIMENT: This could be a reason why people like being around you, with you, and supporting you. Genuine, authentic compliments make people feel good because you are positively taking notice. This is a skill that can be worked on but cannot be faked. False or blurred compliments will not do you or the other person right in the long term.

CONGRATULATE: People work hard for accomplishments, achievements, and much more. Whenever there is something to congratulate, do it.

CONSOLE: A true friend and companion is there when needed. If someone is sick, feeling alone, or going through a tough time, a true friend shows up! Phone calls, random thoughtful messages, active listening, and hugs may be needed to succeed with this value.

Happiness

COMMUNICATE: A GPS provides directions to get from Point A to Point B, and humans also need direction in life. It's essential to express how you feel (whether it's positive or negative – to a certain extent), which will help give direction going forward.

CURIOSITY: Life is an adventure with plenty to explore. It's important to dig into your curiosity to help keep things fun and interesting, and it creates opportunities for extraordinary experiences.

CHARITY: Giving back to things you believe in, trust, and are passionate about will help ensure fulfillment, respect, and gratitude.

What's one thing you can do to work on these four pillars?

_____

_____

_____

***

Completing Your Bucket List Starts with This Story

If you're fortunate enough to live on this planet, why not take advantage and live life up?

What are twenty-five things you'd like to do in your life?

Take time to finish, refine, and put serious thought into this list. Then write them down and cross them off as each one gets achieved!

The best way to get started on a list of tasks is to write them down…

My Bucket List

1.)

2.)

3.)

4.)

5.)

6.)

7.)

8.)

9.)

10.)

11.)

12.)

13.)

14.)

15.)

16.)

17.)

18.)

19.)

20.)

21.)

22.)

23.)

24.)

25.)

Enjoy!

FINAL THOUGHTS

The entire message of this book is to get you thinking of various ways to…

Create Opportunities for yourself and others in all aspects of life (Health, Wealth, Relationships, and Happiness).

Live a positive **Active Lifestyle** through words and actions.

Understand **Respect Is Earned** and not always just given.

Excel Forward to get where you want in life.

…and to help give reason and direction to take action because, when you C.A.R.E., life is a heck of a lot more fun.

My email is bgaydorus@gmail.com, and I'm happy to answer any questions you may have and will be open to any feedback.

If you like the message of the C.A.R.E. Principle, please leave a review and help spread the word!

GIVING CREDIT WHERE IT'S DUE

Thomas Plummer

This book would not have happened if it wasn't for Thom's guidance. Thom is a friend, mentor, and business/life coach of mine. He helped me put together the format and mindset to write "The C.A.R.E. Principle."

Ken Charpentier

Ken has had a tremendous impact on my life, specifically with how to treat people. At twenty years old, working on Cape Cod for the summer, I was looking for guidance on my next step in life. Ken was one of my bosses. He didn't tell me where to go with my life; instead, he led by example and helped me figure things out. Ken taught me the value of being loyal and taking care of people.

The Entire Team at Mike Boyle Strength & Conditioning

Having gone there for a three-month internship in the summer of 2014, I was shocked that my main takeaways had nothing to do with fitness. Which were, learn from people smarter than you to get where you want faster, and how to have fun while still being productive.

Ryan Carroll and Travis Grisham

In the summer/fall of 2015, I worked for Ryan and Travis at The Everglades Golf Club in Palm Beach, Florida. They took the time to teach me how to take initiative, how to own up to my mistakes and fix them, and the importance of communicating clearly.

Brian Gaffney

Brian was another boss of mine who did a great job of leading by example. He taught me the importance of details, dressing like a professional, and, most important, how to treat people with respect. He is a guy who could motivate you without saying a word.

Grant Cardone

Although I have never met Grant, he has taught me the importance of thinking big, building your network, and making things happen in life through his social media posts, growth conferences, and Cardone University.

Steven Covey

Covey's book *Primary Greatness* increased my motivation to write this book. Some of his concepts were mentioned in this book, including the idea of "Creating Your Own University" and his definition of leadership.

Jerry Weintraub

His book *When I Stop Talking, You'll Know I Am Dead* has had more influence on my life than any other book. It's the best book I've ever read, and it influences the way I look at many things in life. Most importantly, he taught me the value of being persistent.

Coach Michael Burt and Eric White

When you meet these two guys, they give you 100% attention, look you in the eye, and treat you with respect. I've gained a lot of respect for these guys over the years and have been fortunate enough to meet both of them. Coach Burt's concepts have had a significant influence on the

"Excel Forward" part of this book.

Lou Miller

Lou came to my college to speak and changed the way I looked at learning. He made me realize that, if you want to learn, you should go right to the top. The "Creating Your Own University" story is dedicated to his concepts and life experiences.

Tai Lopez

Tai is another guy who emphasizes learning from the best. In his *67 Step Program*, he laid down a solid foundation of what successful people do well, which got me believing I could be successful if I put in the work. Tai's concepts have had a positive influence on this book and have led me to meet some great people.

Jim Rohn

Jim was one of the first; if not the first virtual mentor I started learning from. He got me to think big and realize that it is possible to do great things in life. My biggest takeaway from Jim has always been the art of asking, which is touched on toward the beginning of the book.

Jesse Itzler

Jesse is a guy that I found out about toward the beginning of 2019. Once I heard his story, I felt like he was someone I've known my whole life. His "Build Your Life Resume" concepts have had a significant influence on the lifestyle part of this book.

Alex Merrill

Alex has taught me the importance of making people feel welcome, working with a team, and the importance of giving back. He has had a tremendous influence on many of the mentor stories in this book.

Todd Durkin

Todd is energetic, enthusiastic, and impactful. He has taught me the importance of helping people and bringing energy. Todd's dad taught him the life is precious quote mentioned in the "Feeling Trapped, What Do I Do?" story.

Ed Mylett

Ed is another guy I have never met, but he has taught me a lot through his speaking engagements, "The Ed Mylett Show," and through social media. He is one of the best listeners I have ever seen, and he influenced the "Meeting the Person You Want to Be" story.

Andy Frisella

Andy has taught me the importance of taking daily action and doing things the right way. I probably would not have had the discipline and commitment to write this book if it wasn't for his "Win the Day" formula.

Chris Finn

Chris is a good friend and one of my business coaches. He has consistently supported me over the years and is a great role model for "The C.A.R.E. Principle."

Anthony Renna

Anthony is a mentor of mine who has helped me expand the vision of my business and understand people better. He is a great role model for one of the more important concepts of this book, "Create opportunities for yourself and others."

Precision Nutrition

This is a company I have a tremendous amount of respect for. It is a health and wellness company doing things the right way. They have helped me understand the importance of leading by example and being understanding of people's situations.

Alex Morton

Alex has had a significant influence on my passion for writing books. In his mid-twenties, he came out with a best-selling book, *Dorm Room, to Millionaire*. His concepts and life experiences had a significant impact on many of the stories in this book, especially the "Breakfast with Your Mentor" story.

The Greenwich Library

This is a place that has felt like a second home over the last three-to-four years. It's one of the top libraries in the world and has helped me expand my knowledge tremendously.

The Books – *How to Win Friends and Influence People* by Dale Carnegie and *The Obstacle Is The Way* by Ryan Holiday

These have influenced the format and the reason why I wrote this book. I owe them both a big thank you.

The Book – *The Five Love Languages* by Gary Chapman

This is my favorite book on relationships. The principles in it have allowed me to understand people better and to improve my relationships. His concepts have had a major influence on the story, "Becoming a Better Future Boyfriend, Girlfriend, Husband, or Wife."

Steve Harvey

Steve was someone whom I saw speak while writing this book, and I loved the concepts he talked about. He's mentioned in this book, and I appreciate what he is doing for the world.

Jerry Hogge & The Methodist University Staff

These were some of the first people who started giving me opportunities to grow outside of the classroom. Many of the experiences and opportunities I've had would not have been possible without Methodist University. I will always thank Jerry Hogge for consistently telling me about the books he was reading. Instead of telling me to read more, he would say to me what he liked about the books he was reading, which made me more curious about books and the benefits they could bring.

My Mastermind Buddies…
Haylin Alpert & Evan Roehm

I have been fortunate enough to have Mastermind sessions separately with these two for an extended period of time. Whether they are in person or over the phone, it always seems like we end the conversations having learned something new.

My Clients

It would be tough to mention all of them. But these are the people I see weekly who continue to push me to do more, be better, and give back. I've learned a lot from them in various ways, and I owe them a big thank you for their continued support and confidence in me.

The People I've Met Along the Way

I've met a lot of people before and during the writing of this book who have influenced many of the stories. Writing this book made me curious about getting to know people better, which led to some fantastic conversations with couples, roommates, random people on the street, new and long-time friends, and many others. I thank you all for your time, thoughts, and willingness to share some of your experiences with me.

My Family

Their support means a lot and is truly appreciated. Mom and Dad, thanks for always having my back. To my brother (Matt) and sister (Danielle), thank you for being there to listen and help me out with various things in life. To my cousin Kenny, you helped me change my mindset after a setback in 2017 and encouraged me to keep pursuing my dream. It meant a lot to me and significantly impacted my desire to put *The C.A.R.E. Principle* in writing!

THANK YOU FOR READING!

Made in the USA
Monee, IL
29 January 2020